Competitive Tennis for Youn

Produced in English with the financial assistance of the

MANFRED GROSSER
RICHARD SCHÖNBORN

COMPETITIVE TENNIS
FOR YOUNG PLAYERS

THE ROAD TO BECOMING A TOP PLAYER

- IMMEDIATE PROBLEMS
- PHYSIOLOGICAL/BIOLOGICAL DEVELOPMENT
- PERFORMANCE ABILITY AND CAPACITY
- LONG-TERM PERFORMANCE DEVELOPMENT
- PROBLEMS INVOLVING TALENT

Meyer & Meyer Sport

Original title: Leistungstennis mit Kindern und Jugendlichen
Aachen: Meyer und Meyer Verlag, 2001
Translated by Ulrich Hansen
Additional Editing by Phyl Edwards

British Library Cataloguing in Publication Data
A catalogue for this book is available from the British Library

Grosser/Schönborn:
Competitive Tennis for Young Players
– Oxford: Meyer und Meyer, (UK) Ltd., 2002
ISBN 1-84126-075-4

© 2002 by Meyer & Meyer Sport (UK) Ltd.
Aachen, Adelaide, Auckland, Budapest, Graz, Johannesburg,
Miami, Olten (CH), Oxford, Singapore, Toronto

Member of the World
Sports Publishers' Association
www.w-s-p-a.org

Printed and bound by Druckerei Vimperk, AG
ISBN 1-84126-075-4
E-Mail: verlag@m-m-sports.com
www.m-m-sports.com

CONTENTS

CONTENTS

Throughout this book, the pronouns he, she, him, her and so on are interchangeable and intended to be inclusive of both men and women. It is important in sport, as elsewhere, that men and women have equal status and opportuntities.

Fig. 1: Pete Sampras, the best tennis player in the history of tennis, is also a model athlete.

FOREWORD

MANY ROADS LEAD TOWARD ACHIEVING A SPECIFIC GOAL. BUT IS THERE A BEST ROAD TOWARD BECOMING A TOP-TEN TENNIS PLAYER?

Manfred Grosser and Richard Schönborn have faced this difficult question many times and as a result have undertaken a detailed analysis of the demands, particularly on young players who participate in modern high-level tennis. The outcome of their research is this book, which in terms of its breadth of coverage, has no rival. Not only does it cover the entire biological and psychological development of children and young people but it also shows clearly – relative to the level of development of the top-class adolescent athlete – the type, frequency and level of intensity in which training for the top-class adolescent athlete should take place.

This book brings together the results of scientific research and studies, in addition to many years' experience on the part of both authors and various other experts on tennis for children and young people.

The outcome is this indispensable practical guide for parents, coaches and others with an interest in high-level tennis for young players.

If the written rules and regulations of the game are considered then the possibility exists that children and young people can, within their inherent abilities and with their talent, combined with age-coordinated training, achieve their individual optimal competitive limit. This may mean that at some stage in the near future a "new tennis star is born". What this book provides is clear guidelines for coaches and others on how to predict and counteract the problems of early setback of a "great" promising talent brought about by too intense physical demands, false ambitions within the player's family and coaches, plus the use of inappropriate training methods will become a thing of the past.

Having said this the authors make no definite promises that those who read and implement this work will achieve overnight success at the top level.

Dr. Georg von Waldenfels
President, German Tennis Federation

PREFACE – TENNIS TODAY

In the last two decades the sport of tennis world-wide has experienced a tremendous development. It is true to say that while in certain traditional tennis nations there is an air of stagnation, a tremendous development is taking place in so-called third-world tennis countries. It's encouraging to see the return of several traditional South-American nations onto the world stage. Thereby, players, both male and female, who come from countries truly not belonging to the best-known tennis nations, have played themselves into the group of the world's best.

The international top-notch tennis scene has, through total professionalism, entered performance spheres and heights which young up-coming players can only reach through tremendous hard work. This means that the

Fig. 2: The rise to fame is only possible through versatile preparation.

development of a potential young top player has to be planned in a much more conscientious, systematic and more goal oriented manner, if he is ever to have a chance of success. Improvising, unprofessional preparation, false ambition and a wrong set of goals during adolescence will inevitably lead to a lack of success.

The player's individual potential will not be achieved and therefore his highest possible point of performance will not be reached. Many tennis coaches have, unfortunately, missed the new developments in training method. The world's best players are usually those who have been lucky enough to have worked with such specialized coaches. Such players experience the highest performance development within the most favorable time frame for improvement, namely between the age of twenty and about twenty-five. The overwhelming majority, however, stagnate in their development during this decisive period. This is usually the result of several

Fig. 3: Serena Williams is an outstanding example of a meticulous and systematic long-term physical and technical development program during adolescence.

factors, and gives reason to the necessity to become involved with the development of an up-coming potential top-notch player and to systematically clarify and solve problems as early as possible, in order to provide trainers, parents and players with practicable documents which will allow a player, within the limits of his inherent abilities, to reach his individual level of top class performance. This book will help coaches and others to accomplish this.

The authors of this book have decades of successful work both on a national and international basis in the areas of general and specific methodology of training and the science of sports. Through their extensive experience they would like to help prospective candidates for possible top positions in various ranking lists, but above all, the people working with them on the optimal path to success. Having said this even this cannot be a guarantee of success; but is an indispensable prerequisite to the training of top class players.

1 PREMATURE FAILURE – BURN-OUT, DROP-OUT

1.1 ———————————— BURN-OUT, DROP-OUT

Top tennis and above all, world top tennis, gives the misleading impression of players living in a world of glitter success. Sadly many parents, coaches and officials misjudge the reality of this situation due to their lack of understanding of the true realities.

Big money, fame and popularity characterize top players, but they overlook the painful reality of thousands of would-be stars who strive in vain to obtain a place in the heights of tennis, but who are condemned to play only in lower-ranked tournaments and qualifying rounds.

Why is this so? How are some players better capable than others to work at the top level? This can be the result of a questionable attitude toward the game, a lack of mental toughness, un-favourable athletic environmental conditions, poor parental or coaching decisions or the lack of basic training. For the reasons previously discussed it is very difficult to find the absolute correct "medicine", although even here a "remedy" can be found, depending upon an early intervention of expert professionals.

This last statement is based on the premise that with modern knowledge, at least not in those countries in which sport science is no longer a wallflower subject, which is the case in most well known traditional tennis nations, this situation should occur only rarely.

Yet still, the lack of success of numerous young talented players within typical tennis nations is no exception, it is a bitter reality. The few who have made it should not blind us to this reality.

Fig. 4: A situation doomed to failure. A negative surrounding influence (parents, sports officials, coaches) can have disastrous consequences for a talented child.

REASONS
1.2

SUGGESTED REASONS

Permanent lack of success, however, or a very average curve of success is not the only problem. We should be much more worried about the failure quota of young players predicted to have tremendous potential for success or of those who are already very successful, who for various reasons sooner or later experience their so-called "burn-out" (being mentally and physically overstrained, overheated) resulting in the "drop-out" (withdrawal from competitive sports) from top-class competitive tennis. Some try a comeback, but up to now, no one other than Jennifer Capriati has succeeded.

"Drop-outs" like Tracy Austin, Andrea Jäger, Kathy Horwath, Carling Basset, Chanda Rubin, Jimmy Arias or Aaron Krickstein and many, many more became well known and famous through their early or premature success. On the other hand, how many talents have been lost in the sport of tennis who didn't even have time to become successful and famous and who are only known to a small circle within their immediate vicinity. Their numbers go into the hundreds if not thousands worldwide. All show the same causal relationship: too early a start in top-class competitive tennis, beginning at the age of 14-16, thereby having a totally insufficient physical, mental and long-term technical and systematic development during adolescence, a requirement for future top performance in such a complex field of sports like tennis. After three to four years they all experience their downfall.

THE TRUE REASONS

Other than the above mentioned reasons, what are the true reasons for a "burn-out" with the concomitant "drop-out" at such a young age?

Next to generally understandable reasons like:
- Insufficient talent
- Inability to cope with top-class competitive stress
- The importance of other priorities, for example professional training/ university education
- Participation in other sports

However, two reasons are decisive:

1. The player is, in spite of high physical talent, not well enough prepared for constant performance at the top level. This is largely based on insufficient, long-term general and specific training in physical conditioning and technique, This leads to continuous rising physical overload resulting in an increasing number of injuries, interruptions to training sessions and tournaments and finally to more and more discontent, and less and less success, finally leading to an ultimate physical breakdown. Simplified one can say, that because of the player's enormous talent and pure technical capabilities he is able to play in a league for which he does not yet have the necessary physical stamina.

2. Through the premature introduction to the world of top tennis he is under such psychological stress that he is not yet able to cope with this pressure with regard to his own expectations as well as the expectations coming from external sources such as parents and or coaches.

The following aspects are covered in detail in this text:
- General stress
- Long-term pressure to achieve top-class results
- Long-term pressure to take part in matches
- Too many seasonal peaks
- Training extent and intensity too high
- Too frequent anaerobic lactic strains
- Not enough time for regeneration and recovery
- Insufficient physical training
- Lack of general and specific conditioning
- Conflict with aggressive opponents, with coaches, parents and officials
- Inability to adapt sufficiently well to the different stresses imposed
- Unexpected defeats – great victories in the beginning cannot be repeated

A child and a junior are not small and middle sized adults respectively. A child remains a child and a junior is a junior with all their varied biological, physical and mental components. One would, for example, not expect a leading position in business from a seventeen-year-old. In tennis, however, the public expect from an athlete of this age that he is physically, mentally and technically an adult and consequently at the level of top players. Certainly there are always exceptions to the rule, which occurs more often in women's tennis, where several adolescents have accelerated in their development, and are therefore far ahead of their age group. That, however, should never be used as a scale of measurement for the large number of talents. It is always advised to be on the side of caution when entering top tennis, because top-class competitive tennis can on the average be played only about ten years. Around the age of twenty-five the player reaches an individual performance peak, which can then be held for only a few years. (Cf. also Fig. 36. p.117).

DIAGNOSING BURN-OUT
1.3

The question of what causes burn-out is a difficult one to answer. Given the fact, that if the correct training methods are used such problems should never arise during adolescence. However, should this situation occur it is important that it is recognized as early as possible. At the first signs of an upcoming "burn-out", adults working with the player should use counter measures in order to prevent a "drop-out", thereby making it possible for the player to continue his career.

As a rule, the following warning signs appear by the majority of the players separately or accumulated:
- High general sensitivity
- Impatience
- Weariness
- Rejection of ideas and suggestions
- Obstinacy
- Frustration
- Seeing no sense in one's work
- Physical fatigue and exhaustion
- Rising number of injuries on account of excessive physical demands and increased different infections caused by a weakened immune system

Such symptoms are the last warning signals; the often made call for the use of extreme common sense, and calling on the player greater self-sacrificing, more concentration, to work harder are completely unnecessary. This only pulls the players deeper into their predicament.

1.4   SUGGESTED SOLUTIONS

In such a situation one must remember that the player is "sick and tired", which means that it is virtually impossible to motivate him in a positive manner. He finds himself in a condition, which anyone else in any other profession can experience; namely exhausted, worn-out and at the end of his strength. The only solution is to take a rest, stop playing, and take a vacation, regenerate, in the hope of affecting the healing process and starting afresh.

Fig. 5: As long as tennis is fun, there's hardly any danger of experiencing a "burn-out" or "drop-out".

1. The first step in the regeneration process is to stop all tennis activities. No training, no tournaments; in fact a total disengagement for at least 6-8 weeks. During this time the player should turn to those activities that he most likes, the activities he missed while playing tennis. He should avoid all forms of stress; one can say he should drop out for a short-term period. Should sickness or injuries have occurred, then these should be completely cured before returning to the sport.

2. Once the reasons for the "burn-out" have been found and the actual situation is recognized, a long-term systematic and gradual build-up process lasting from a number of weeks up to several months, without tournament stress should be carried out.

3. Following such an incident as described above it is very important to stress that the player must not be allowed to act in the same manner as before, otherwise, within a short period of time, he will fall into the same rut as before. This phase in particular can be decisive on whether or not the player can be led in the right direction or if his final "drop-out" phase is inevitable.

4. A change of coaches is normal under such a situation, but if the original coach not only finds out the exact reasons but also possesses the ability and professional knowledge to fit the training program and tournament plan onto the new demands and goals, given that he still retains the player's confidence, then he should continue to work with him.

5. The change within an athletic environment is the most decisive factor in the 'cure' of burn-out. Under certain circumstances, parents, officials, the club, friends and others should be included notwithstanding the fact they had an earlier negative influence and contributed to the so-called "burn-out". Given that they accept their responsibility and agree to change in their behavior there is no reason why they should not make a positive contribution to the player's future development.

6. **By far the best solution is not to let such problems arise in the first place.**

Fig. 6: Marat Safin plays that modern aggressive tennis of the future. In his youth he already possesses tremendous technical and above all physical requirements.

2 BIOLOGICAL PERFORMANCE ABILITY AND LOAD CAPACITY DURING CHILDHOOD AND ADOLESCENCE

2.1 THE PROBLEMS INVOLVED IN SYSTEMATIC LONG-TERM DEVELOPMENT

The following section is proposed as a scientifically based, long-term systematic path of development of future champions between the ages of 5 and 17.

A systematic long-term performance programme from the early years up to the beginning of top-class competitive tennis extends over a period of between 8-5 years (for more details see p. 71).

Throughout the support and development of tennis talent, from the beginning it is important to acknowledge fairly unpalatable fact, namely that the physical condition of children and adolescents is getting worse from generation to generation. In Germany for example, "statistically 65% of the children in primary school have posture weaknesses or even injuries" (GROSSER/STARISCHKA [7]1998, 176). Therefore, not only parental upbringing falls under scrutiny but also physical education in schools where, with few exceptions, much remedial work has to be done. That means that lack of physical fitness and other weaknesses influence the work of sport clubs, including tennis coaching and thereby present a first big obstacle in a child's development. This means that the tennis coach must not only concentrate on the technical development but also on the total coordination training and physical conditioning of his student within his daily training program. Long-term athletic training is an indispensable prerequisite for a successful future career in sports! This demands that the responsible coaches within such long-term and systematic training don't just create the necessary organizational and technical training, in conjunction with parents and officials. Additionally, they should know the different phases of development with the concomitant limitations imposed by each phase and use these to develop a strong, agile, skillful player, who if he has the ability will be prepared to compete at the highest level.

A basic knowledge of fitness and technique training are therefore far from being the major knowledge base on which the coach must draw. One needs to know in regard to what, when and how a young player will react in an optimal manner, which areas must be emphasized at any given age group and, most importantly, why a specific outcome occurs. Therefore it is necessary to understand and explain the scientific results regarding the biological and motor development of young people.

BIOLOGICAL DEVELOPMENT FROM CHILDHOOD TO ADULTHOOD
2.2

"Base knowledge of biological development is absolutely necessary for all instructors, physical education teachers and coaches for a better understanding of:

Starting with age 4-6, growth and development patterns, motor capabilities and therefore the correct timing to start the training of the indispensable bases of individual (and complex) fitness levels, ensuring muscular balance; in addition to recognizing the balance between technique and fitness training (also physical strength) and finally the short-, middle- and long-term control of the total performance."

(GROSSER/STARISCHKA [7]1998, 177)

BIOLOGICAL DEVELOPMENT

For the successful training of young players, the different biological phases of development during his period of growth have to be respected. Every training session, and training phase, makes a relatively high demand on the player's organs (meaning disturbance of the inner equilibrium, the so-called homeostasis) it is through this disturbance of homeostasis that changes in the organism are effected. For example, this may be coordination, metabolic and structural adaptations to various organs/central nervous system, muscular system, cardiovascular system, skeletal system, hormone system, immune system etc. The organism always reacts in keeping with its innate capacity and ability to adapt. Which is dependent upon the actual and biological age, sex, training condition and other factors. The training stimulus, for example, that can be optimally tolerated by a 17-year-old junior player would have a negative effect on a 10-year-old player. On the other hand, certain areas can rarely be developed in an optimal manner in later years. Therefore, if they are neglected during childhood, certain conditions of motor (biological) development determine the quality and quantity of the adaptation brought about through training and tournaments.

"...Under motor development, one understands a process of changes in physical dispositions (physical attributes and abilities) brought about through talent and environmental influences. For the sport, predominantly fitting components of motor (biological) development are growth and coordinative and conditional abilities..."

(GROSSER/STARISCHKA [7]1998, 178).

Growth itself relates to height and weight and all inner parts of the individual. On the following pages we will explain more closely the periods of growth of selected physical systems.

GROWTH SPURTS

The period of time from birth to adulthood can, roughly speaking, be divided into calendar sections of the so-called width and length growth spurts shown in Table 1.

Life Section (Age period)	Calendar/chronological age	Growth
Newly born	up to 3rd month	beginning width period parallel to first length growth spurt
infant baby	4th to approx. 12th month	
infant	2nd and 3rd year	
early childhood (pre-school age)	4th to 6th/7th year	
middle childhood (early grammar school age)	6th/7th up to 9th/10th year	
late childhood (late grammar school age)	10th/11th year of age up to puberty (girls 11th/12th, boys 12th/13th year)	second width growth spurt
early adolescence (pubescence, 1. pubertal phase)	girls 11th/12th up to 13th/14th year, of age boys 12th/13th year up to 14th/15th year	second length growth period
late adolescence (adolescence, 2. pubertal phase)	girls 13th/14th up to 17th/18th year of age, boys 14th/15th up to 18th/19th year	third width growth spurt
Adulthood	Following	

Table 1: Periods of calendar age and growth (in the style of ASMUS 1991, 168)

The stages of growth shown in calendar form are obviously to be looked at as flowing. Development takes place in stages. Explanations in calendar form serve merely as considerations and applications to training (see also "growth peculiarities", p.35).

Within phases of growth, strong individual differences can be observed due to acceleration and retardation appearances, also between boys and girls. That is why the so-called "biological age" is of more importance for a performance-oriented development than the actual chronological age.

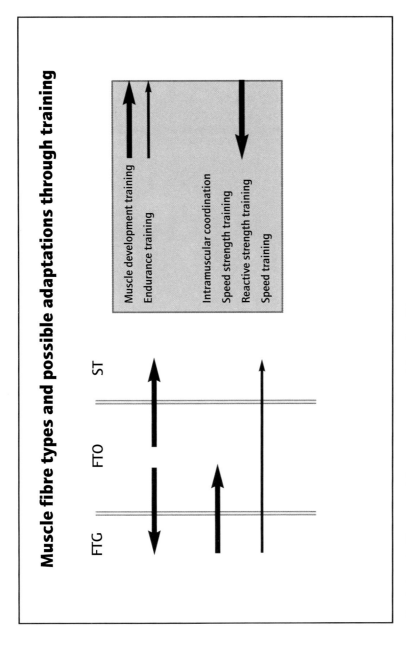

Fig. 7: Muscle fibre types (also compare text p. 26 and 57ff.)

THE GROWTH OF THE CENTRAL NERVOUS SYSTEM

From the first day of birth, brain cells begin to connect themselves to form certain motor patterns. By about 6 years, the human brain has developed to approx. 90% of its final size and the nerve conducting processes between central nervous system and muscles have now matured. By the age of twelve, the brain, with its approx. 100-300 billion cells, has reached its final size.

It is well-known that the brain is the centre governing motor coordination and speed. Therefore, the ages between 6/7 and 12/13 present biologically ideal conditions for performance development of coordination, movements/techniques and speed of reaction, all factors that play a tremendous influence on performance in tennis! (for further evidence of the special importance compare also p.48).

IMPORTANT FOR COACHES: The ages between 6 and 13 are considered the best "motor learning ages" and here, coordination, speed of reaction, action and frequency plus tennis technique should be given absolute priority in the training program because the formation of new neuronal connections (motor programs or engrams) are established. Therefore the training of all basic techniques should be completed between the ages of 11–13.

THE GROWTH OF THE ACTIVE MOTOR SYSTEM

The term active motor system in this context refers to the skeletal muscular system. Not only are there quantitative differences between the muscles of both male and female but also quantitative and qualitative differences exist between children and adults. These exist on the basis of genetic premises, also partially between the same age group of the same sex.

Basically, skeletal muscle is divided into two different types: Fast-Twitch-Fibres (FT) that divide into so-called "FTO" (oxidative character – rapid contraction) and "FTG" (glycolytic character – very rapid contraction), and the slowly contracting Slow-Twitch-Fibres (ST) (compare also Fig. 7, p.25)

The division in percentage terms in the average person is 40% FTG, 20% FTO and 40% ST fibres. However, genetically, strong deviations of up to 80% in one direction exist (so-called "born sprinters" or endurance athletes). Independent of his genetic make up man is born with non-specific differentiated muscle. During the time of puberty the genetically conditioned division of muscle fibres finally attains full growth.

Even a 12-year-old child's slow twitch fibres stand at approx. 65-75% of their ultimate structure. For this reason, systematic endurance training during the child age of 6-12/13 years is not recommended because most children already have a sufficiently natural endurance capability, achieved by playing normal regular sports. Beyond this, quality endurance training demands much training time, which is not normally available during childhood or results in a loss of training of other necessary factors (see above).

With regard to body weight, the development of muscle mass by children and adolescents is illustrated in Table 2 below.

> 4-6 years	approx. 20% of the body's own weight
> 7-10 years	approx. 23% of the body's own weight
> 10-12/13 years	approx. 25-28% of the body's own weight
> 12/13-14/15 years	approx. 30-35% of the body's own weight
> up to approx. 16/19 years	approx. 33-45% of the body's own weight

Table 2: Age divisions and muscle proportion (from GROSSER/STARISCHKA [7]1998, 179)

IMPORTANT FOR COACHES: On the basis of only a small muscle mass (primarily with 4-13 year-olds) existing, purposeful muscle training is absolutely necessary. Adaptations at this age are given through improvements in the intra- and inter-muscular areas of coordination as also in the growth of muscle length and through aerobic capacity. Starting at the time of puberty a purposeful muscle development program is rewarding (and necessary!).

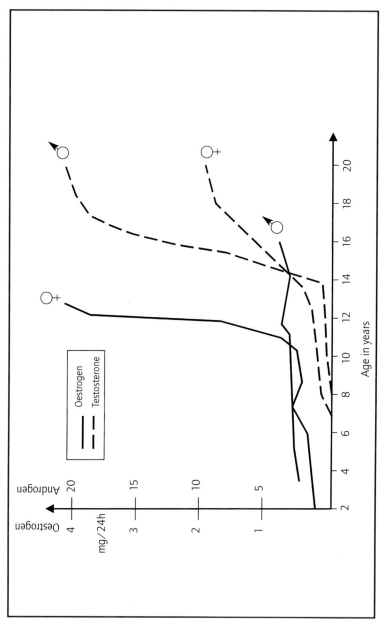

Fig. 8: The formation of testosterone and oestrogen by boys and girls during age development (from: KOINZER 1987,209)

THE GROWTH OF THE HORMONAL SYSTEM

The sexual hormones oestrogen (feminine) and androgen (masculine; esp. testosterone) are extremely low in children up to the 10th/12th year, then, however, their production climbs very rapidly (see Fig. 8). It is known that the androgen testosterone is biologically responsible, among other things, for an increase in muscle growth, which by the time of puberty shows itself more in boys than girls, particularly with regard to muscle mass and strength capabilities.

IMPORTANT FOR COACHES: Through this simple biological fact it is possible to draw one's conclusions concerning the content and effect of training in the different age groups.

As mentioned in the previous chapter concerning muscle mass and the increase of testosterone, significant muscle development training at the age of puberty and finally in the second phase of puberty is meaningful and rewarding.

THE GROWTH OF THE PASSIVE MOTOR SYSTEM

The passive motor or skeletal system is, during childhood and the adolescent period, considered to be one of the weakest and therefore most fragile systems of the human organism (compare Fig. 9). For this reason, the system has to receive special attention throughout the training process. Injuries occurring during adolescence through intensive workloads are often the reasons for later "Drop- outs" occurring. Continuous performance stagnation and increasing injuries to top-notch players also occur.

N.B. Girls reach full skeletal maturity at the age of 19, boys at the age of 21.

IMPORTANT FOR COACHES: To stop possible injuries before they happen it is absolutely necessary to develop as early as possible, a so-called "muscle corset". Therefore, using the proper dosage "functional muscle training with children, starting approx. at the age of 8 years, is an absolute must" (GROSSER/STARISCHKA [7] 1998, 179).

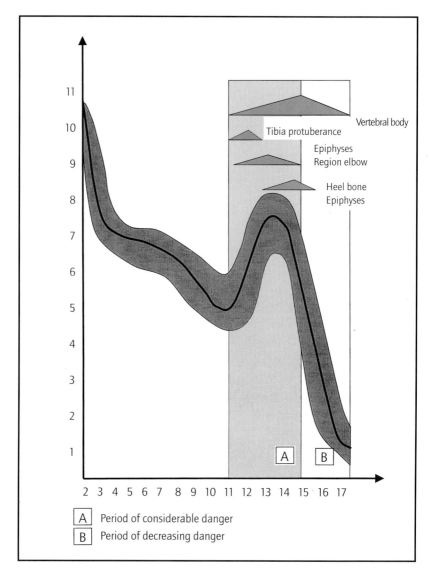

Fig. 9: Special danger periods for a maturing bone of especially loaded areas with girls; this period appears with boys approx. 2 years later (from FRÖHNER 1993, 61)

Discussions of muscular training are intended to cover the general strengthening and the improvement of muscular elasticity, as well as the prevention of a possible muscular imbalance. Especially in tennis, a comparatively one-sided (bodily) sport, this is of supreme importance!

THE GROWTH OF METABOLISM

For all children, and especially athletic children, **nutrient metabolism** is of utmost importance. It controls all the structures, changes and developments of the body. Children have an approximately 25% higher basic metabolism than adults and therefore need more vitamins, minerals, nutrients and protein.

*"...If the **catabolic metabolism** is not sufficient to assure extreme load, then this can result in system modification (compare for example, the apparent smallness of children taking part in gymnastics!)..."*

(GROSSER/STARISCHKA [7] 1998, 180).

In tennis, the bodily load during childhood is not as high as in gymnasts, but through systematic training high enough to cause deficits in nutrient metabolism if the catabolic metabolism is under too much exhausting pressure. That is why it is especially important to pay attention to adequate nutrition fitting to the player's age and athletic capabilities, it is also important to ensure an adequate regeneration process.

The importance of this precaution rises with age because the biological processes at puberty, combined with continuously increasing bodily load and growing intensity of training, which in addition to playing tournaments, demands a high metabolic capacity.

The aerobic metabolism is well developed by the time a player is 8 years old. This means that the physiological parameters of aerobic energy available, such as the VO_2max, the cardiovascular system, blood volume, mitochondria, enzymes, the oxidation rate of free fatty acids, carbohydrate reservoir etc. reach, relatively speaking, the value of adults (compare also Fig. 10, p. 33).

IMPORTANT FOR COACHES: Isolated endurance training in 6-12-year-olds is not necessary. If the children are healthy no endurance problems should arise. This means that they cannot only cope with longer lasting highly intensive load but also less intensive loads of short duration, (compare also Fig. 11 p. 34). As opposed to this, the anaerobic metabolism at a child's age is still extremely low. The reasons being the low phosphate reservoir in the muscular cells as also the reduced ability to produce and eliminate the production of lactate. For this reason training methods, with children between the ages of 6-12/13, should be of be high intensity but long-range work should be avoided. Children are not biologically in the position to work well under anaerobic lactate conditions. This means, also the tennis technique exercising and training methods MUST be carefully planned. For example, long rallies with twenty and more repetitions (HOPMANN drills) should not be practiced at this age. Beyond this, children's bodies show a poor blood circulation to the internal organs and skin when taking part in intensive load programs. This in the end leads to a reduction of the performance ability and also require an extension of the regeneration process.

THE GROWTH OF THE IMMUNE SYSTEM

The immune system is fully matured by approximately 17 years of age. Setting load scales and intensities too high and having insufficient time to recover means the player will be more prone to illnesses, which is not only dangerous to the player but also leads to training interruptions and causes a drop in performance. **Here, the philosophy "Less is more!" is appropriate.** Through an increased need of oxygen by the body, that – caused by increasing work loads – reaches a peak of ten to twenty times of the initial level, and through changed blood streams in the body's circulation system, the so-called "free radicals" are produced and released. Fighting these aggressive materials reduces the power of the immune system, making it easy for viruses to attack. This is one reason why so many injuries occur, particularly in top players, where one expects them to be immune to such minor injuries because of the training they receive.

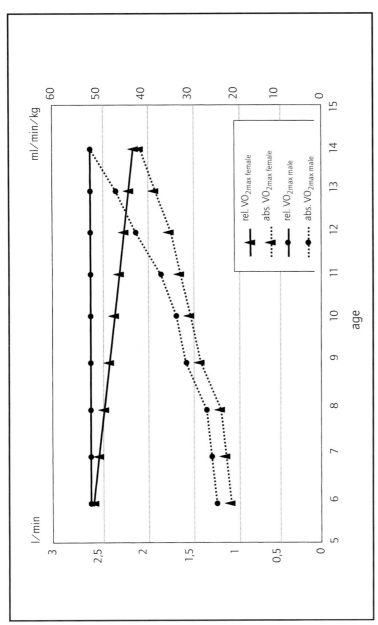

Fig. 10: Mean value of the absolute and relative VO$_2$max with girls and boys during childhood and adolescence (after ROWLAND 1990, p. 258).

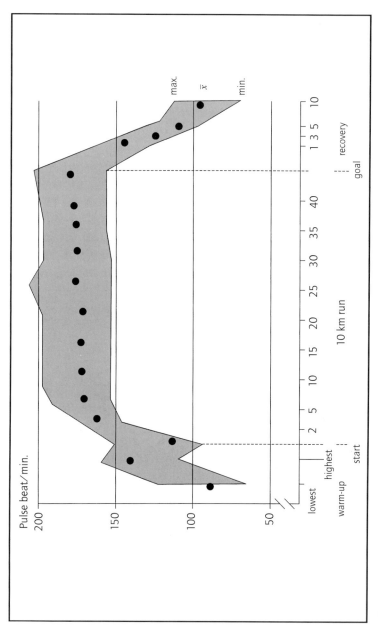

Fig. 11: Graphic description of heart frequencies of trained school children in the early and later school age, before, during and after a 10 km run (BUSCHMANN 1986, 36)

THE GROWTH OF THERMO-REGULATION

In moderate climatic conditions children, in comparison to adults, show no thermo-regulated differences. Under extreme climatic conditions they have the following deficits: a higher mass metabolic turnover rate, which means, children produce more metabolic heat per kilogram of their body weight. Furthermore, children have an inadequate blood circulation to their internal organs and skin, through intensive load programs, leading to a reduction of their long-term endurance.

THE DEVELOPMENT OF SPECIFIC GROWTH

Next to the chronological age (i.e. the individual's true age) it is also possible to differentiate using the so-called biological age (i.e. as measured by the current stage of physical growth and development). For example; 13-year-olds can be either accelerated, which means, related to their age group they are taller, heavier and thereby have more strength and endurance of, let's say a 15 year old, or are retarded in their physical development, meaning they are below the norm of their chronological age (for example gymnasts; compare also Fig. 12 and 13). One often mistakenly sees in the accelerated children much too prematurely defined talents. Physically retarded children can of course catch up to or pass the normal and accelerated individuals during their childhood development.

A SUMMARY OF DEVELOPMENT AND FITNESS DURING CHILDHOOD AND ADOLESCENCE

If one compares the different **components of growth in their development** the following aspects can be summarized (compare also Fig. 14 p. 38):

- The growth curves of the **nervous, cardiovascular** and **muscular systems** show a regular rate of increase, whereby the nervous system reaches its full maturity before all others (between the 12th/13th year). These three systems hardly make excessive demands upon the children. Relative to the adult population they "shift" back by themselves in case of high physical exertion, meaning they cannot voluntarily stress themselves as much as adults.

- The developmental curve of the **skeletal system** and the **psyche** show a bend in the first pubertal phase, which indicates problems with both factors in this period. The skeletal system is still a weak point in the complex organism, in fact it could be called the weakest link in the chain.

- Children, strangely enough, feel no fatigue in their skeletal system through high load capacities and as a result there may possibly be some small damage occurring in the area of the joints, the capsules, the cartilages and the spinal column. These damages are not even registered by children. The whole skeletal system is still very soft at this age and is thereby able to act as a shock absorber and adapt itself. The accumulation of not registered micro-traumas over a long period of time may lead to damage, first showing itself during adolescence and at the latest, during adulthood. Health problems that top-class players also have in this area, do not, as a rule, come only through top-class training or extreme pressure during matches. The organism was simply not prepared for the heavy load capacities of top-class tennis or possibly had a hidden injury already.

- The bend in the curve of the psyche is a sign that **mental problems** exist, which develop within the first pubertal phase resulting from hormonal changes that occur among the major number of adolescents. Different interests, understanding life better, the influence of the opposite sex, new group of friends, a desire to rebel, an extreme tendency toward fashion, etc., lead to growing problems on the tennis court.

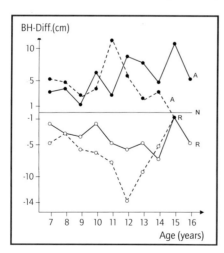

Fig. 12: Deviational diagram of body height of early (A) and late developers (R), compared with normally developed (N) (accord. to WUTSCHERK et. Al. 1985, 144).

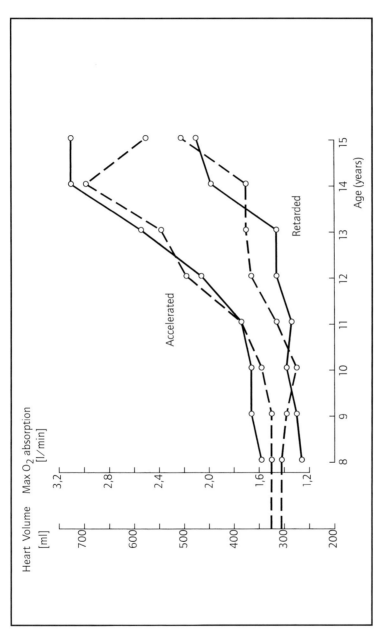

Fig. 13: Cardiac volume and maximum absorption of oxygen (as a gross criteria of endurance performance ability) by accelerated and physically retarded adolescents between 8 and 15 years of age (accord. to HOLLMANN et al. 1983, 12).

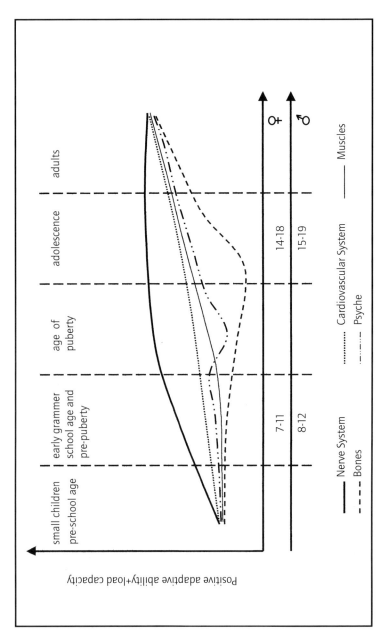

Fig. 14: Schematic representation of the development of the load capacity of the biological systems being dependent upon the biological age (from: FRÖHNER 1993, 17).

Here, the coach needs a sensitive touch and patience and thereby has to find and use the right coaching method. Normally, this period in time is rather short, lasting only a few months and in the worst case roughly one to two years. It is, however, a very critical period that can lead to giving up the game or to a lack of interest in competitive sports. The problem should not be dramatized but also not underestimated.

In Table 3 (p. 69) the development of important motor components is again presented in an overall view. Furthermore, the development course of motoric abilities as well as training contents are shown during childhood and adolescence.

DISCUSSION: MENTAL AND COGNITIVE DEVELOPMENT OF CHILDREN AND ADOLESCENTS

It is self-evident that thinking, intelligence and especially the mind or mental aspects play an important role in athletic performance. If one looks at the development of children and adolescents it is possible to observe four pillars of development: the cognitive, the mental, the social and motor development. In addition to the above mentioned motoric biological area, we will also examine the cognitive and mental process.

Man's development is based upon his desire to achieve harmony between himself and his environment. In the individual stages of development, children and adolescents adapt better mentally and cognitively to one another through their activity in the environment and through genetic conditions. Regarding the cognitive and psychological stages of development we still quote PIAGET (1972) who formulated the following four phases:

1. **The "sensory-motoric phase" i.e. the first two years,** where the child has the first experience with its sensory organs and its motor system, so that dexterity of movement develops.

2. **From the 3rd to the 8th year of age, the so-called "preoperational thinking" phase,** the child develops mental impressions regarding his actions, however, in a simple form with simple rules and focused on material thinking. In addition, the child shows strong egocentricity, partially also differentiated interests and tendency toward self-evaluation.

3. **With approximately 7/8 years the third phase** begins. Here a change from a mental development to a more logical form of thinking takes place, especially at the end of the phase around the 13th year. Explicit operations now replace the predominant intellectual egocentricity. Children now develop a stronger personal autonomy and a much more highly developed motoric and social behaviour – important for team structure and tactical understanding. A strengthening of the ability to concentrate and anticipate develops as well as the strengthening of the own will. Children at this age find themselves in a very good state of mental equilibrium and therefore accept assignments without criticism.

4. **Around the age of 13 stage 4 begins.** To win, think and feel, a stage that on the one hand is meant to be cognitive and concrete at the same time, but on the other hand has little equilibrium because of emotional surges and inner conflicts taking place. Discrepancies between reality and the overestimation of one's own abilities often occur. Perseverance (for training) and the will to succeed (in tournaments) are not strong.
Nevertheless, the adolescent tries, on the basis of his gradually stronger developing cognitive performances and his strengthening mental capabilities, to find an inner harmony and mental balance on his way into the world of adulthood.

LOAD CAPACITY AND PERFORMANCE ABILITY
DURING CHILDHOOD AND ADOLESCENCE
2.3

THE UNITY OF LOAD CAPACITY AND PERFORMANCE ABILITY

"During physical performance it is essential to understand the totality of the individual physical make up of the athlete", i.e. that which makes it possible for him to cope with the demands of movement learning and training. The specific physical systems involved are coordination, strength, speed, flexibility and endurance plus technique. All of these are based upon the level of sophistication of the individual's motor characteristics (see above), in that the child or young adult is only capable of certain load capacities that can be

developed, for example, through tournament training exercises. As the performance ability of its weakest link limits this it is important that this factor is known and understood/accepted by both coach and athletes. Load capacity, itself, is cf. FRÖHNER (1997, p.55) is an essential characteristic of the individual and because of the complex aspect of the biological systems that are dependent upon general health for the ultimate level of development. Furthermore, it can be affected by external influences such as nutrition, lifestyle and the method and intensity of the current work load"

(GROSSER/STARISCHKA [7]1998, 181).

Based on the previous chapter, and again in the following chapter, it is necessary to make the reader aware through practical examples of the similarities and differences of performance ability and load capacity:

- During childhood and adolescence, adverse affects on the developing bony structure often occur through the effect of high **mechanical loads** upon the individual, which can lead to longer breaks in training or to a drop-off in the performance programme. This is why the influence upon the skeletal system and the ligament structure through mechanical load has to be carefully monitored.

- If not taken into account and not recognized as important, **deviations from the norm** within a delicate system, especially during childhood and adolescence, can signal a reduced load capacity of the support and motor system that can be the cause of enormous negative consequences at a later period. This despite there being a high performance level.

- "Characteristics of load capacity differentiate strongly in **comparison to characteristics of athlete performance**. Some conditions, which at first appear advantageous for performance, in the course of the performance development may cause health problems. An example is the extreme mobility of hyper-mobile children with soft connecting tissue" (GROSSER/STARISCHKA [7]1998, 181; cf. also supplement Fig. 15, p. 43).

If one, more specifically, **lists the requirements and necessities of loads in training and competition** by children and youths, the following aspects are important:

- Setting of general and sport-specific goals.
- Establishing a long-term (approx. 10 years) systematic development plan.
- Taking into account the optimal effect of the set training stimuli, which means age-specific intensities, training methods, processes and goals, which respect the stage of biological development.
- The establishment of age-specific loads which are adapted to suit each individual, this means that the given stage of development, state of adaptation and the general health of the individual have to be taken into consideration.
- A training program that puts the complexity of training as being of prime importance.
- Of providing the highest quality training all the time.
- Of providing training that is fun and motivates; playful and competitive forms are preferred.
- The necessary periods of regeneration must be planned and kept up.
- The player's health must always be of greatest importance.
- The nutrition must guarantee for the replacement of lost energy and comply with age-specific and athletic demands.
- The level of performance should not be predominantly judged according to tournament results but mainly through the achieved athletic performance level and development rates of performance during training. In fact judged on the basis of individual improvement in all faces of training and competition.

IMPORTANT FOR COACHES: The key to an optimal path of athletic performance development of young people is concerned with:
- The complexity of training, and
- The continuous monitoring, and/or eliminating existing or possible newly appearing weak points (e.g. weakness in specific muscle groups have a direct effect upon inter-muscular coordination processes and these determine, as we well know, technique development).

This is why, from the beginning, the **complex view** of the athletic performance ability and **highly complex training** are the decisive factors. In fact they are **the key** to everything!

Finally, only along this path it is possible to develop a general and specific level and maintain optimal performance.

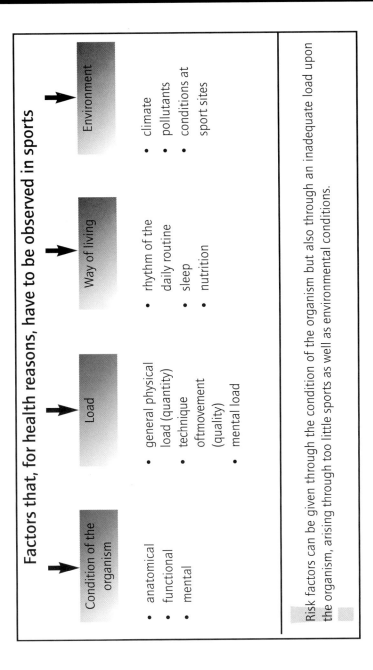

Factors that, for health reasons, have to be observed in sports

Condition of the organism
- anatomical
- functional
- mental

Load
- general physical load (quantity)
- technique of movement (quality)
- mental load

Way of living
- rhythm of the daily routine
- sleep
- nutrition

Environment
- climate
- pollutants
- conditions at sport sites

Risk factors can be given through the condition of the organism but also through an inadequate load upon the organism, arising through too little sports as well as environmental conditions.

Fig. 15: Important factors for a good health in sports. An orientation for spotting risk factors (from: FRÖHNER 1993, 90)

WHICH COMPONENTS DETERMINE THE PERFORMANCE ABILITY IN TENNIS

Before heading toward complex or difficult physical work for example, conditioning work on a short-, middle- or long-term basis, as in all other sports it is necessary in tennis to first of all gather knowledge of the **discipline structure** and requirements, in other words, those factors that will affect performance in a positive or negative direction. In particular (compare also Fig. 16 and the annotation on p. 46):

- which motor goals and techniques does tennis demand?
- which physiological, time-oriented and
- which anatomic and mechanical loads and strains occur?
- which mental abilities are necessary?

Only through this knowledge a scientifically based performance control during training and competition will this be possible.

In the following paragraphs **selected test data** will be discussed.

- Although a tennis match can last over five hours, the loads during the separate rallies (points) are, on the average, very short. For men, they lie between 2.7 s. on grass and 6.5 s. on hard courts and 8.3 s. on clay-courts. For women, they lie between 5.4 s., 6.6 s. and 10,7 s. Between these time ranges only, on the average of 2.1, 5.1 and 6.8 strokes per rally take place. That means that a player only has 1.05, 2.55 and 3.4 strokes available on these three different playing surfaces in order to make a point! Women have about 1.8 to 5 strokes available to make a point. It is possible to imagine the type of quality of these few available strokes to make the major number of points and win the match.
- On hard courts, 79% of all points are made at the latest with the sixth stroke (the third for one player). On clay, 62% of all points are decided upon with the sixth stroke.

This shows that service and return, taken together, within 62-79% of all cases, make up one-third of all strokes made! Therefore on hard courts, 37-42% of all points are won at the latest after the return has been made. On clay, 30-33% are won after the return.

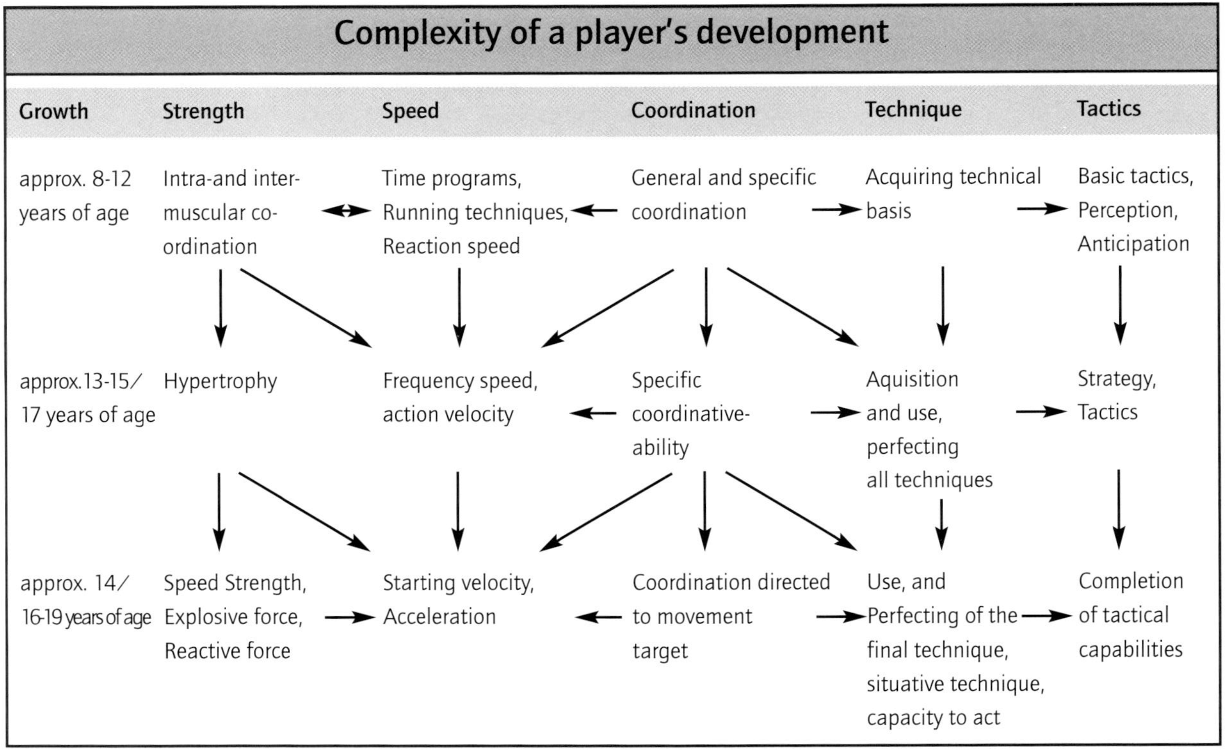

Complexity of a player's development

Growth	Strength	Speed	Coordination	Technique	Tactics
approx. 8-12 years of age	Intra-and inter-muscular co-ordination	Time programs, Running techniques, Reaction speed	General and specific coordination	Acquiring technical basis	Basic tactics, Perception, Anticipation
approx. 13-15/ 17 years of age	Hypertrophy	Frequency speed, action velocity	Specific coordinative-ability	Aquisition and use, perfecting all techniques	Strategy, Tactics
approx. 14/ 16-19 years of age	Speed Strength, Explosive force, Reactive force	Starting velocity, Acceleration	Coordination directed to movement target	Use, and Perfecting of the final technique, situative technique, capacity to act	Completion of tactical capabilities

Fig. 16: Overall view of the complexity of a player's development (accord. To SCHÖNBORN 1999)

Note to Fig. 16:
The figure shows the individual emphasis, as well as the connection, and/or mutual influence of the individual components during the complex training of the player within the three decisive age periods.

From childhood up to becoming a top-notch-player the central role of the neurological system is recognizable. Individual coordination has a very strong influence upon all forms of speed, as well as on tennis technique. Both of these aspects need to be carefully developed throughout the total training period. Therefore, systematic general and specific coordination training plays a decisive influence upon the performance development of a tennis player.

Beyond that, age-specific strength development has a very special significance because it not only has strong influence upon stroke force capabilities but also upon acceleration at short sprinting distances. Reaching the ultimate goal of technical development in tennis and thereby fulfilling the prerequisites for a maximum level of performance – perfecting all techniques and having the optimal ability to act – is not possible without following a systematic development of all the determining components of performance.

WHAT CONCLUSIONS CAN BE DRAWN?

First of all, during a rally the short-term physical loads mean that tennis, is mainly an **anaerobic-alactic sport.** The major energy deliverers are hereby the so-called "fast" (immediately available) phosphates ATP (Adenosintriphosphate) and CP (Creatine phosphate) that have an enormous effect upon training extents and intensities.

Because the storage capacity of these phosphates, during maximum working intensity, is relatively short (approx. 5-10 secs.), relative short rallies (approx. 5-20 strokes) should be played, which are combined with regeneration intervals of approx. 15-25 secs. In order to guarantee **high intensity** while keeping up a **high quality in the training** of tennis strokes constitutes the provision for acquiring fast and precise strokes, which again are a requirement to end rallies fast and successfully.

Today, ball velocities of 190-220 km/h by services and 100-130 km/h by winners, returns and passing shots are reached. In order to reach these velocities and to cope with them successfully, a player needs, in addition to excellent perceptual processes and ability to anticipate, a highly developed coordination, frequency speed, speed or reaction, speed of action, reactive-power, explosive power, speed strength, he also requires the ability to achieve equilibrium, to orientate, to adjust and to differentiate.

The spatial dimensions of the court are fixed in scale and therefore the longest **running distance** on the court straight on amounts to at the most 14-15 m. Usually, during a rally of two strokes, distances between 3-7 m are covered, certainly, under certain circumstances theses are repeated one after another and very fast. That again means that explosive power, reactive power, speed strength (acceleration) and frequency speed are of utmost importance for the lower extremities.

For the necessary **perfection of legwork** in all difficult situations (e.g. by return-ball, passing-ball or lob) optimal coordination, speed of action and ability to maintain equilibrium, are an absolute prerequisite.

Although, during a three-set match the player only covers a **total distance** of approx. 1300-2500 m, and approx. 2400-4000 m during a five-set match these are done in short bursts with adequate pauses in between of 25 s, therefore the aerobic capacity of endurance is also of vital importance to the tennis player. This not only determines the length of the optimal load capacity during the match and during training, but also the time and quality of regeneration between points, between tournament days and matches and within and between the individual training units and days training.

As already mentioned, the ability to **perceive and to anticipate** are additional performance determining components that can only be achieved through storing numerous similar situations in memory. This means that these situations have to appear not only during matches, but as importantly during training!

The **psychological sphere** covers a wide area of performance enhancing and limiting components. Included in this sphere are factors such as motivation, self-confidence, striving towards personal goals, level of aspiration, will, mental toughness, self-control, independence, flexibility of thought, the ability to concentrate, to take in much information, and to digest and to store this information, playing the game with wit and flair, and much more. All these areas have to be continuously developed and promoted during long-term training.

All the examples cited make clear that the training toward becoming a top player demands a long-term, systematically planned and above all complex training programme. Today no coach can build up top-class or a world-class player through flair and improvisation alone, it is essential to have first class professional knowledge.

On the following pages are covered the important performance areas such as technique, force, speed, flexibility and stamina (for the training itself, cf. pages 71ff. and the appropriate literature references).

MOTOR COORDINATION AND MOTOR TECHNIQUES

Under the "coordination" factor within the motor process, it is necessary to have, from a practical athletic point of view, the orderly connection of different parts of movement. Physiologically speaking the working together of the central nervous system and the skeletal muscles (inter and intra muscular coordination), that is functionally and anatomically correct, the cooperation of agonists, synergists and antagonists, as well as from a biomechanical point of view, the agreement between inner (=muscles) and outer forces (e.g. gravity).

Correct coordination is required for the successful implementation of the following: movement time, movement velocity, movement strength, motor economy, precision and consistency, amplitude of movement plus any problems which might arise during movement production.

This must be taken into account when considering the demands made on the player in establishing a specific goal that he is striving to achieve. The above factors play a large part in determining the quality of an excellent tennis technique (cf. SCHÖNBORN, 1999). This means, the quality and

Fig. 17: Tommy Haas, from his youth on, experienced a systematic development in the USA.

number of different skills the player brings to the game early in life will later influence the potential level of the player's playing ability. The better the quality of coordination, the much more direct, less difficult and more precise will the performance goal be achieved. As the motor process becomes more flexible, the level of fatigue is lowered.

The ability to intuitively gain precise control of the movement gives the player game stability and the necessary capacity to perform. Because tennis is a sport which in a single situation requires not only different game components at the same time, but through which several simultaneous phases of movement, different processes of coordination take place. (For example, during a tennis stroke more than 100 muscles are involved). Within the in game coordination processes this is what is known as "motor complexity". Thereby, the transfer of the conditioning components into the tennis technique is only possible through excellent coordination.

Through these examples it must be obvious how important the buildup of coordination is for a tennis player. Because coordination is mediated through the central nervous system (CNS), the optimal period for the development of this factor is during that phase of life during which the brain is still in the process of development, but has already reached a level of maturity, which guarantees a high quality in the process of performance and storage.

Again, as was made clear in the previous chapter, this is the period of life between approx. 6-7 and 11-13 years of age. Therefore, coordination training represents a major point of emphasis in the training volume of this age period (cf. also fig. 18).

With reference to **coordination training** the following important aspects are to be considered:
- Contents of each session
- Physical load possibilities
- Perceptual conditions
- Conditions of mental pressure

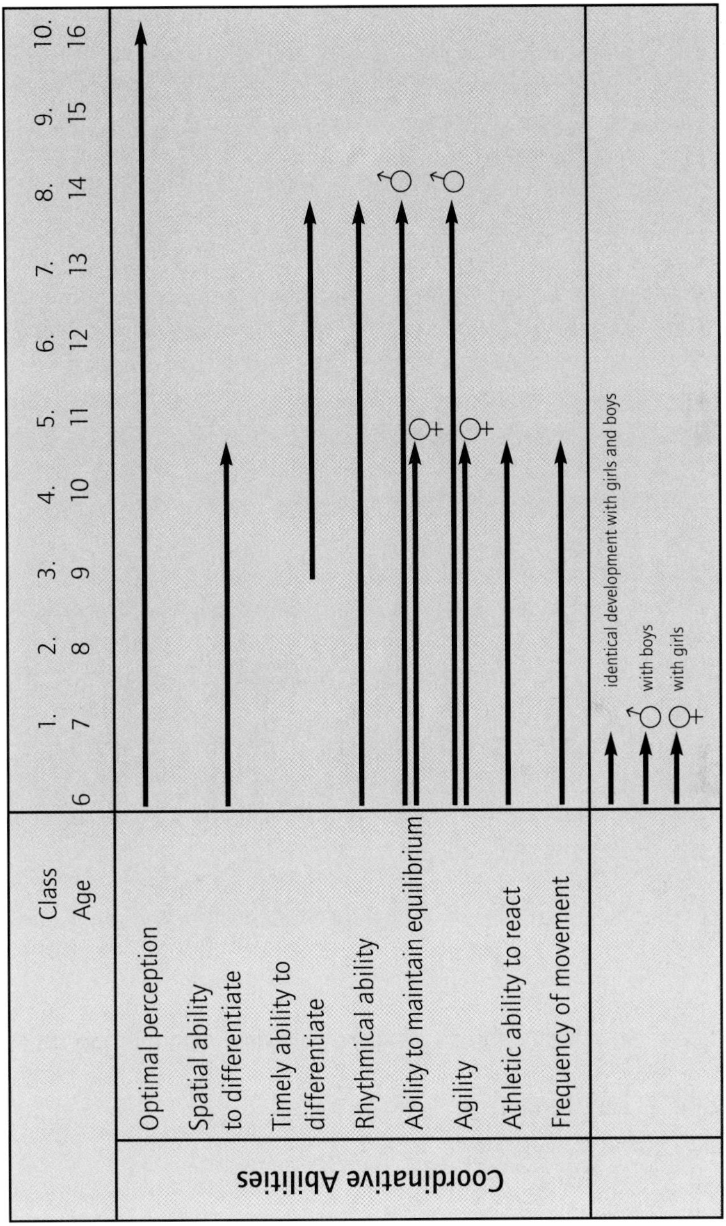

Class	1.	2.	3.	4.	5.	6.	7.	8.	9.	10.
Age	6	7	8	9	10	11	12	13	14	15	16

Coordinative Abilities

- Optimal perception
- Spatial ability to differentiate
- Timely ability to differentiate
- Rhythmical ability
- Ability to maintain equilibrium
- Agility
- Athletic ability to react
- Frequency of movement

Legend:
- identical development with girls and boys
- ♂ with boys
- ♀ with girls

Fig. 18: Phases of intensive development of selected coordinative abilities during childhood and adolescence (see HIRTZ 1985)

1. With regard to **content, coordination training** at this age level should show variety, because it is necessary to build a large repertoire of movement skills. Through the learning of movement at the level of the neuron, through biochemical means, connections of brain cells, so-called „engrams" are developed and the more comprehensive they are, the better they can later be transferred to the situation of the game during the match. Also other abilities, as for example the ability to maintain equilibrium or jumping strength, which is trained in various ball-sports (football, basketball, hockey...), also whole-body exercises (e.g. judo...) can be ideally transferred to situations of movement in training and in matches. A similarity exists in ball-throwing movements, which, from a biomechanical and coordination point of view, support stroke production in tennis.

2. The aspect of **physical load** plays a role, because the central nervous system controls the course of the coordination process and, thereby, signs of fatigue within the system have a direct negative effect upon the quality of coordination. Without the player being aware the central nervous system in physiological terms tires before the muscles, and it is usually through a drop in playing quality that such a situation is recognizable. This means that coordination work must be highly intensive but short and has to be filled with many regenerating breaks. Long periods of time without a break would be very unfavourable.

3. With regard to **conditions of perception and pressure**, one has to say that playing situations in tennis demand more than just a "clean" stroke technique learned under easy conditions. On the contrary, as already mentioned, during a game it constantly depends upon the production of techniques under different playing conditions. These techniques have to be perceived as fast as a flash (through the player's sensory organs), thereby putting more or less high mental pressure upon him. Seen under these conditions, technique training must relate to its use in the game, after a certain phase of learning the basic structures of movement should be taught by variable training. This, in training science is called "technical application training" or more recently "coordination training".

This coordination training consists of already learned basic techniques plus perceptual situations in addition to conditions of mental pressure" (cf. also NEUMAIER 1999).

Obviously the coordination training should not end at the age of 13, on the contrary, it must continue systematically and progressed with a specific end point in mind. This is especially true during puberty, when temporary disturbances in coordination can be brought about by strong growth developments, which should be negated through good training; the same also applies to other age levels. Only the contents and goals change with time and adapt to the respective age and playing quality of the player.

Practical instructions to increase coordination:
- Increasing the demands for precision resulting in increased pressure for precision
- Increasing execution speed
- Increasing time pressure for motor action.
- Increasing demands of complexity, for example through undertaking additional exercises, binding movement into a motor combination, through the addition of a given load, etc.
- Practice under variable environmental conditions, which demand a continuous adaptation of movement within changing surroundings (i.e. increasing the situation pressure).
- Taking up fitness handicaps or combining with demanding conditioning exercises and additional mental demands.
- Change of distance and intervals, beginning or end position, direction of movement or goal, of employment, of strength and similar aspects.

Especially in the successful achievements on the tennis court, it is possible to see the decisive differences between an absolute top player and an average one.

REFERENCE

In the mean time, numerous publications, textbooks, videos etc. are on the market that present numerous general and tennis specific, practical coordination exercises for all ages, for example "Advanced Techniques for Competitive Tennis".

(SCHÖNBORN, 1999)

SPEED

Speed in athletes is defined as the ability, through "cognitive processes, a strong-will and the function of the nerve-muscle-system to achieve maximum reaction speed and movement velocity under definite given conditions"

(GROSSER 1991, 13).

Complex speed can be subdivided on the basis of scientific knowledge and practical experience into the external appearance, reaction time plus simple and complex speed ability.

The **elementary speed abilities** are exclusively determined through the so-called "time programs" meaning high-grade neuro-muscular control and regulatory process. A high share of fast twitch muscle fibres (FTG/FTO fibres) in combination with the specific technique of movement and against little resistance is a major determinant of speed.

With regard to the appearance of movement, one has to differentiate speed of reaction for a-cyclic movements and frequency speed for cyclical movements. It is generally accepted that pure speed is very largely genetically determined.

Complex speed ability is concerned with motor performance, which, next to biological facts of elementary abilities, is also based largely upon explosive and reactive strength and/or specific endurance (anaerobic-lactic energy availability). Here also, one differentiates between a-cyclic (strength speed and strength speed endurance) and cyclical forms (sprint force/accelerative ability and sprint endurance).

Fig. 19: Venus Williams dashed into the worlds peak by playing a hard tennis without compromises, something she already learned in her youth.

All types of speed in tennis, aside from the endurance forms, are of extreme significance. Modern Tennis is characterized through its enormous ball velocity. Serves of over 200 km/h are normal, even in women's tennis. Strokes from the base line, above all winners and passing balls, but also returns, are being hit with velocities of far over 100 km/h. In order to reach these balls, the player needs, next to abilities to perceive and to anticipate, excellent reaction abilities, starting and explosive abilities.

Since the central nervous system controls the major part of speed, it establishes for the biological (and training) purposes the development of elementary speed abilities in parallel with that of coordination: this is best covered during the highest growth rates, viz between the ages of 7-12 years.

"Children of this age (10-12 years) possess such a high so-called plasticity of the central nervous system, which on the one hand means a high irritability of the nerve control processes and on the other hand a still weak differentiating inhibition. The high irritability, however, is the reason for fast reactions, favourable for the implementation of time based programmes and also simply the ability simply to acquire movement skills"

(GROSSER/STARISCHKA [7]1998, 211).

With increasing age (11-15 with girls and 13-17 with boys), the influence of the strength region is increased through hormone distribution (testosterone and oestrogen; cf. Fig. 8, p. 28) and the thereby caused muscular growth (growth of muscle fibre length and cross section enlargement). The differentiation of the FT fibres upon the development of speed rises tremendously, which manifests itself above all in the jumping power. That is why it makes sense to begin the training of this form of speed with the beginning of and not before the pubertal phase has begun.

During speed training, the quality of the technical performance of individual forms of movement stands as being of paramount importance. Through wrong technical processes, "wrong" patterns are stored in the brain (e.g. a poor running and throwing technique) that can later strongly limit an optimal development of speed.

Also, the intensity of execution is decisive; through the just mentioned technical training of the new motor processes the execution should take place within a middle range of intensity so that the young people should help facilitate the understanding of the correct motor processes. If the technique is right, one always has to train with a very high intensity (90-110%), which means that the player is basically moving at a maximum performance level.

REFERENCE:
For individual forms of speed training we recommend the book "Speed Training for Tennis".
(GROSSER/KRAFT/SCHÖNBORN 2000).

STRENGTH

Without strength, athletic performance cannot be realized. Especially fast motor processes (in tennis, serves, spurts etc.) are dependent upon a highly developed explosive strength.

By definition, strength is seen as *"The ability of the nerve muscle system, through enervation and metabolic processes involved in muscular contractions, to overcome resistance (concentric work), to counteract (eccentric work) and/or to hold resistance (static work)"*
(GROSSER/STARISCHKA [7]1998, 40).

On the basis of scientific knowledge and given facts, one differentiates the **complex strength**, into
• Maximal strength which is seen as a basis strength for:
• Explosive power and power with additionally
• Reactive strength and also
• Strength endurance

The **biological factors that influence the development** of strength are partially similar to those for speed, i.e. genetically based, especially those called upon for maximum speed movements. This refers to, among others, the number of Fast Twitch fibres as well as the enervation ability (contraction

Fig. 20: Nicolas Kiefer came into the world's top playing class through a systematic development training program over a period of many years, offered by the Lower-Saxony Tennis Association and the Bundesleistungszentrum (Federal German Training Centre) of the German Tennis Federation in Hanover.

speed) and special reflex mechanisms. Other influencing factors like the cross-section, reactive tension ability (stiffness), intra- and inter-muscular coordinating ability, and anaerobic-a-lactic and lactic metabolism as also an optimal starting and pre-stretching length are developed by training

In the early and later school child age (approx. 6-12 years) the centre of strength training lies at puberty and above all in the adolescence age period. This does not mean, however, that children between the 7/8th and 11/13th year of age should not do strength training. The opposite is true at this age, where the already explained skeletal instability as also weaknesses of stance, attributed to muscular unbalance, are found with children.

The so-called "posture muscles" (in certain positions, e.g. upper and lower back muscles, hip muscles, breast and oblique muscles) are neglected with most children. Through the functional muscles, not only the normal, daily exercise but also the natural growth of the extremities, leads to an adaptation of the responsible muscles, resulting in an relative increase in strength, which is so decisive for young athletes.

A *"weakening of the posture muscles stands for reduced functional control of the total muscular system and in the long run, an overloading of the passive motor system (bones, joints). A targeted programme of muscular development, seems, for this reason, compellingly necessary (it is well known that an improved strength level leads to an improved motor control)"*
(GROSSER/STARISCHKA [7] 1998, 186).

During strength training within childhood and adolescence, the establishment of a dynamic working method stands in the foreground, whereby:
- **By the age of 8-12 years,** muscular development plus natural growth in length of the muscle fibres, through an intra- and inter-muscular coordination, as well as an improvement of metabolism (and thereby the so-called relative strength) is given. Intra-muscular coordination is the so-called sequencing and recruiting of the motor units. Sequencing is the gradation of the impulse frequency. Recruiting means the inclusion of a certain number of motor units during a contraction. Both are dependent

upon training (cf. negative example Fig. 21). The goals of muscle training of this age group are non-specific basic training for all muscle groups and the improvement of speed strength. Possible training activities: working out at different ball sports, little games, judo, skating, etc., as also carrying out special strength programs designed specifically for this age group (e.g. see GROSSER/STARISCHKA [7]1998).

- **At age 13/14,** biologically, androgen and oestrogen are produced that lead to protein-anabolic effects (muscle hypertrophy). The goals of muscle training are, increasing power and the start of actual muscle development. The training program now encompasses predominantly exercising programmes relating to all muscle groups (consisting of strength and stretching exercises) (e.g. see GROSSER/STARISCHKA [7]1998).

- **During adolescence, starting at 14/15 with girls and 16/17 with boys,** the young figure comes to maturity and, therefore, the highest phase of strength training can now begin, whereby, it is important to consider in practice, that the skeletal system reaches its full development with girls at the age of approx. 18/19 and with boys at approx. 19-22.

REFERENCE:
Further detailed explanations and training programs can be found in: GROSSER/KRAFT/SCHÖNBORN: Speed Training for Tennis, Oxford, 2000.

Fig. 21: By no means should strength training look like this with 8-12 year olds. At this age intra- and inter-muscular coordinative ability should stand in the foreground of training.

ENDURANCE

Endurance means, generally, the ability to resist a tiring load physically and mentally for a long time, and/or to recover quickly from physical and mental demands. Training for a longer period of time affects consequently mainly endurance sports, while the ability to recover rapidly between and after loads is important for non-endurance sports like tennis.

In sports, one differentiates between basic endurance and special endurance. Only the first type is particularly important for tennis. **Endurance is no performance determining factor in tennis** but rather a supplementary factor which becomes noticeable in the quality of training and when playing tournaments, through the ability of the player to recover and to regenerate within only a short-time period. This is guaranteed through a good basic endurance (aerobic energy availability VO_2max rel. of approx. 60 ml).

Fig. 22: Latin America is coming back. Many national associations have developed new youth programs in whose development one of the authors participated to a very large degree. Nicolas Lapentti is only one of many new young talents.

TRAINING

- Endurance training for tennis playing 6-12 year olds, on the basis of biological (although suitable!) conditions (e.g. p. 31), is not really necessary. The frequency of activities undertaken as part of the training regime at this age level results "automatically" in an increased adaptation in aerobic metabolism.
  Finally, also for time reasons is endurance training unnecessary as the time is better spent on other factors which are more amenable to training.

- The best phase for a rewarding and increased training of the aerobic system is puberty and naturally following, also during adolescence, during which phase the anaerobic-lactic energy availability can be increased.

FLEXIBILITY

Flexibility is characterized through amplitude, which through internal and external force is reached at the final position of joints.

It depends upon the buildup and the natural directions of movement of the joints (=agility) as well as the 'stretchability' of the muscles.

Goals of flexibility training:
- Optimising the elastic nature of muscles and in connection with that
- The development of the necessary force, as well as
- Making use of the anatomically given movement ranges of the joints. In addition
- The improvement of the reflex controlled coordination process of muscles.

One differentiates between general flexibility (for everyday movements) and special flexibility (e.g. hurdlers, women gymnasts etc.)

Basically, optimal flexibility is a requirement for anyone wanting to reach the top in tennis. Without exceptional muscular elasticity, training goals may be difficult to reach in other areas, for example strength, speed, coordination.

Fig. 23: Martina Hingis is an absolute exceptional talent who cannot be used as an example of a model career for junior tennis players.

Additionally, reduced flexibility makes the player more **prone to injury**, motor skill learning for example, the development of tennis techniques are made more difficult and an imbalance in muscular development may occur. An inelastic antagonistic muscular system which should make possible the full freedom of movement of the agonists has a movement restricting effect thereby reducing force and speed and finally the period of muscular generation is extended because the muscles do not work economically.

For these reasons, correct **age-specific flexibility training** is recommended at an early stage and is strongly dependent upon age.

1. **"Children have, up to the age of 10,** a natural well-formed flexibility, whereby at 8/9 years the spinal column has the greatest flexibility. For that anatomical reason no flexibility training is necessary, although some may be included provided it is in a general and playful form.

2. **At the end of the early school age** (approx. 9-10 years), beginning limitations of the ability to spread the hips sideways and the limited dorsal directed (backward) flexibility in the shoulder joint is noticeable with girls and boys.

   Now, flexibility exercises, in order to maintain the players flexibility are necessary. It Is important to begin with specific exercises for all children who participate in top-class competitive sports that demand high flexibility.

3. **Starting with the late school age** (approx. 10-12 years) flexibility can only be maintained or increased in the direction of the movement that is being trained. The major task of flexibility training at the late school age is less the maintaining of certain joint flexibilities (other than in top-class sports) but rather the prevention and/or the equalization of possibly already existing muscle contractions and muscular imbalances.

4. The strong period of growth during **puberty** (with girls, starting with approx. 11/12 years; with boys, starting with approx. 12/14 years) of

about 8-15 cm per year and the simultaneous hormonal change, means partially an unfavorable mechanical movement pattern for young players, combined with limited flexibility.

Purposeful flexibility training is especially necessary for schools (3x per week) and also for top-class sports (possibly daily), also because at this age period increased muscular imbalances (muscle contractions and reductions) can appear. Precaution is also necessary at this age, regarding non-physiological exercises, e.g. hyper flexion and hyperextension forwards and backwards.

"In the adolescent phase (girls starting at approx. 14/16 years; boys starting at approx. 16/17), training forms and methods as used by adults are already appropriate because of the gradual maturing of the muscular and the skeletal system" (cf. GROSSER/STARISCHKA [7]1998, 228-230).

AN OVERALL VIEW OF DEVELOPMENT AND PERFORMANCE LEVEL DURING CHILDHOOD AND ADOLESCENCE

2.4

AT THE BEGINNING THE COMPLEXITY

Children between the ages of 5-8 years i.e. at the beginning of a possible tennis career, naturally show a physically unstable "structure". The major part of their biological development relates – because of the up to 90% matured brain and central nervous system – to a beginning high-grade coordinative ability on the one hand, and – because of the relative small percentage share of muscles in comparison to the total body weight and hereby very "supple" but unstable skeletal system – to higher athletic demands, therefore providing a weak body type.

A FINAL THOUGHT

One very important factor at this age is not to do one sport to the exclusion of all others as this may lead to a "burn-out" or "drop-out" direction.

COMPLEXITY AND COORDINATION SPECIFICS

In the course of development we now come to the age group of **up to 12/13 years.**

- According to our long-term scientifically based training plan, the actual, so-called "basic training" takes place between 6/7 and 9/10 years, the middle of the above mentioned age range.

- As can be seen in Table 3 (p. 69), the age between 6/7 and 12/13 it is still possible to prevent the buildup and development of muscular imbalances. This means that it is necessary to carry out a high-grade complex total physical development programme.

- If the young person has still to continue growing, there still exist excellent conditions for the development of coordination (the central nervous system is fully matured at the end of this stage) and abilities have to fully develop and must be achieved through training.

COMPLEXITY, COORDINATION, CONDITIONED AND TACTICAL SPECIFICS

At puberty (approx. 11-13 years), through hormonal changes, possible mental variations may take place and through increased vertical growth, partial coordinative limitations may occur. These hormonal changes also provide positive biological requirements for growth and the development of anaerobic-lactic energy.

Therefore, in terms of competition **the ages of 11/13 up to 18/19 years** should be developed as follows:

- Continued complex coordination and fitness training because it is still demanded by the biological condition (e.g. also Table 3)
- Continued refining of coordination and technical dexterity (up to virtuosity!)
- Beginning and gradually increasing muscle and endurance training.
- Tactical training and taking part in tournaments start to become more important, whereby, tournament results and rankings should first be seen as a criterion for training.
- Results and performance development become more important in their own right approximately at the age of 14/15 with girls and approx. at the age of 15/16 with boys.

Table 3 explains the information again in a synopsis.

Age	Phase of muscular adaptation	Muscles: strength and flexibility	Metabolism: endurance	Central Nervous System: coordination and speed
6/7-9/10	Preventive and Development phase	• Approx. 23% muscle part • Weak supporting muscles • Little testosterone • "supple" skeletal system • good flexibility	• high heart frequency • approx. 40 ml VO_2 max • starting favorable aerobic metabolic adaptation • unfavorable anaerobic energy supply	• brain growth = 90% • beginning of good movement coordination • reaction and frequency speed
9/10-12/13	Balancing and Development phase	• 25-28% muscle part • little testosterone • still weak skeletal system • muscular imbalances • good inter- and intra-muscular coordination • satisfying flexibility	• 40-48 ml VO_2 max untrained (60 = trained, similar to adults) • unfavorable anaerobic processes with increased catecholamine distribution	• brain fully matured • very good motor-coordination • high reactions and frequencies
12/13-14/16	Stabilizing phase	• approx. 30% muscle part 35% muscle part ♂ ♀ • androgen and oestrogen distributions • unstable skeletal system • limited flexibility	• favorable aerobic processes • gradually better anaerobic processes	• possible coordinative limitations (growth) • favorable strength speed
15/16-18/19	Forcing phase	• approx. 35% muscle part 44% muscle part ♂ ♀ • stabilization of skeletal system • hypertrophic peak • reduced flexibility	• very good aerobic and virtually anaerobic processes	• renewed favorable coordinative abilities • high speed abilities

Table 3: Overall view of the development and performance ability during childhood and adolescence (from GROSSER/STARISCHKA '1998, 182)

69

Fig. 24: Venus WILLIAMS and her sister Serena were kept away from tournaments through their father until the age of 15. Up to that age they were both systematically trained. Their success shows that their path was right.

3 LONG-TERM PERFORMANCE DEVELOPMENT IN TENNIS

STEP-BY-STEP PERFORMANCE DEVELOPMENT AND IMPORTANT TRAINING PRINCIPLES
3.1

Only through the knowledge of biological growth and as a result, the development of different methods of training at different age levels, is it possible to lay down a long-term successful performance development plan.

This development extends over a period of 15-18 years, from 5-7-year-old beginners up to individual top-class performance, which lies around the age of 22-25 with male tennis players (somewhat earlier by women). From a beginner up to a successful professional male or female player one has to calculate a time-span of approx. 8-10 years with girls and approx. 11-13 years with boys. Exceptions are the rule, when some young players reach the peak earlier than others.

Only those, however, who have been meticulously trained in all areas (e.g. the Williams sisters), will be successful for a longer period of time. The destiny of most players is to drop out of the game, the reasons were discussed in chapter 1.

Those who have reached the peak very early should not be seen as a model for others. In each generation there are a few exceptions worldwide. It is possible to subdivide the long-term performance development into the levels shown in Table 4. The detailed contents of tennis training will be discussed in the following chapters (starting with 3.2)

Training level	Age
Versatile basic training	Approx. 4-6/7
Basic training	Approx. 6/7-9/10
Development training 1	Approx. 9/10-11/13
Development training 2	Approx. 11/13-14/15
Connecting training	Approx. 14-16/18
Top-class competitive training	from approx. 16/19
(In several sections up to top-notch performance; age and duration are dependent upon kind of sport)	

Table 4: Steps of a long-term performance development (from GROSSER/ STARISCHKA [7]1998, 183)

TRAINING PRINCIPLES

These are to be seen as guidelines for the performance development during childhood and adolescence. Precisely expressed, training principles are based upon knowledge pertaining to sports science and upon experience from coaches and experts.

They are general guidelines for the controlling (planning and execution) of training (closely following GROSSER/STARISCHKA [7]1998, 18-36 therefore for more refer to this text). Before any planning and implementation of training begins, a so-called guiding principle should be considered.

PRINCIPLE OF DEVELOPMENT AND HEALTH PROMOTION

This states that an athletic training at no time should hamper the physical, mental and/or motor development, but rather promotes and takes into consideration the factor general health through the responsible avoidance or best possible reduction of risks. With the help of fitness training, a wide basis of physical motor performance ability and resistance load capacity can be achieved.

On this basis, an increasingly specialized and performance-oriented training can be carried out. It is very important that the individual's developmental age should always be taken into account.

Table 5 gives an overall view of the training principles within individual training levels.

Training levels	Training principle
Basic training 6/7-9/10 years	• Principle of the effective motor stimulus • Principle of the optimal ratio of load and relaxation • Principle of variations • Principle of age suitability
Development training1 9/10-11/13 years	In addition: • Principle of repetition and continuity • Principle of priority and purposeful coordination
Development training 2 11/13-14/15 years	In addition: • Principle of load increase • Principle of dividing into periods/cycles
Connecting training approx. 14-16/18 years	In addition: • Principle of individuality • Principle of the regulating interaction of individual training elements
Top-class competitive training from approx. 16/19 years	• Principle of cyclical regeneration

Table 5: Training steps and the application of training principles according to the age

73

TRAINING PRINCIPLES OF BASIC TRAINING FOR 6-10-YEAR-OLDS

PRINCIPLE OF THE EFFECTIVE MOTOR STIMULUS

This principle states that training stimulus has to exceed a particular **intensity threshold** in order to achieve an adaptive reaction.

The biological background is the rule of stimuli stages through which, regarding functional and morphological changes of adaptations, subliminal (= under the effective stimulus threshold), supraliminal weak, supraliminal strong and too strong stimuli are differentiated. Subliminal stimuli remain ineffective, supraliminal weak ones maintain the functional level while supraliminal strong ones (= optimal) cause physiological and anatomical changes. Stimuli that are too strong, harm the functions.

PRINCIPLE OF THE OPTIMAL RATIO OF WORKLOAD AND RELAXATION

This principle takes into consideration the fact, that after an effective training load (training unit) a certain time is necessary for the individual to recreate himself in order to carry out a new similar load (next training unit) under favorable conditions. Load and relaxation should be viewed as a whole. The biological result is the **phenomenon of super-compensation**, through which, through the application of a strong load stimulus not only a compensation or re-establishment of the starting level occurs but an overcompensation of the demanded energy storage (Creatine phosphate, glycogen) appears. The increased level does not survive through a one-time load but recedes. On the other hand, it is the phenomenon of the connection between performance ability and fatigue (= two factor theory), which means precisely that after a training load, a rise in fatigue takes place with a simultaneous rise in performance.

PRINCIPLE OF THE VARIATION OF TRAINING LOAD

Within the framework of an effective training load, the role of the **sympathetic vegetative nerve system** must not be overlooked. The sympathetic nervous system sets the body into a state of readiness for high performance, which is a necessary prerequisite for effective training loads. Through continuous similar stimulation, the sympathetic nervous system is subject to the stimulus stage rule and a decrease of its **ergotrope (performance increase)** effect takes place. Similar training stimuli over a longer period of time lead to a stagnation and concomitant fall off in performance. A change in the load stimulus can bring the player back the previous stage of stimulation. This variation must relate within the practical sphere of training, not only to changes in intensity but above all to a change in training contents, dynamics of movement, the organizing of breaks, in other words, training methods. They constitute an **interruption of the load monotony** within the vegetative nervous system and cause, as unusual motor stimuli, additional homeostasis interruptions with subsequent adaptations.

PRINCIPLE OF AGE SUITABILITY

As was mentioned previously, meaningful performance development can only adjust itself according to the biological age (above all the so-called "sensitive phase") and the individual biological circumstances. Physical conditioning, psychosocial and coordination-technical abilities and skills can only receive optimal promotion in this context.

THE ADDITIONAL PRINCIPLES OF DEVELOPMENT TRAINING (1) OF 9-11/13-YEAR-OLDS

PRINCIPLE OF REPETITION AND PERFORMANCE CONTINUITY

To reach an optimal adaptation it is necessary to repeat the load several times in order to achieve stable adaptation, because the organism has to run through a series of radical changes to its functional systems. The final adaptation is reached when not only the enrichment of substrates (= high-

Fig. 25: Marat Safin serving

energy materials) but also adaptations in other functional systems (e.g. enzyme system, hormone system) took place and, above all, that the central nervous system as the leading stage of load performance has adapted itself. It is well known that the metabolic and enzymatic adaptation proceedings are carried out relatively fast (2-3 weeks). Structural (morphological) changes take longer (at least 4-6 weeks).

The steering and regulating structures of the central nervous system need the longest period of adaptation (months). If regular and continuous load stimuli fail to appear, a **retrogression** of the functional and morphological adaptations take place **(de-adaptation)**. By already executed adaptation, stability loss of the control and regulating system occurs.

PRINCIPLE OF PRIORITY AND PURPOSEFUL COORDINATION

In tennis (as in all other sports) the concern is with the priority of individual abilities, either conditional or coordinative. With training it is possible to achieve the dynamic stereotype (goal oriented coordination).

It is however possible to differentiate between the following:
If the priority of a single conditioned factor or ability is necessary (e.g. in tennis, speed strength) it may be necessary to pay attention to the performance control process and supporting abilities to ensure that the development of priority abilities are not neglected (cf. also "principle of regulating interaction"). In tennis these supporting abilities are speed strength, reaction time, flexibility and aerobic endurance (in the sense that the better the regenerative ability and additional increased trainability of the muscles). The trainability of prior conditioned factors demands a broad general basis in tennis and the corresponding (biological) motoric (and psycho-cognitive) developmental position. If the **priority of certain coordinative abilities and/or individual technical motor processes** is necessary, then it has to be considered that within a performance control process, **all** complementary abilities and exercises are to be seen in connection with the prior element.

If, consequently, individual conditioned and/or coordination elements are improved, they must be immediately integrated into the real time a defence structure of the movement to be worked upon. This happens through numerous repetitions of the whole movement, at first with a mean required and/or somewhat reduced velocity, gradually building up to a correct simulation of the shot, as it would be played in a match.

This is achieved by following the steps as outlined below:
- The use of partial elements with immediate integration into the overall movement, whereby the latter is always the most important element in the coaching scenario, or
- Through the complex training of conditioned and coordination factors.

THE ADDITIONAL PRINCIPLES OF DEVELOPMENT TRAINING (2) OF 11/13-15-YEAR-OLDS

PRINCIPLE OF PROGRESSIVE LOAD INCREASE

When training loads remain equal over a long period of time, the player adapts to them and therefore the same load stimuli ceases to become less effective and as a result there will be little likelihood of an increase in performance. The consequences of a progressive increase of the training load over a certain period of time may be twofold.

1. The increase may occur gradually or suddenly depending upon the player's biological age, training age and the level of development of his sport specific skills. The increase in small steps (gradually) always makes sense as long as by using this method an increase in performance is usually achieved. However, if a slight rise of the training load doesn't achieve improved performance then a sudden load increase may be necessary at a high training level.

2. The increase may occur in sudden jumps in training load and intensity (increased possibility of injury, performance instability). If using this method while great care must be taken to avoid injury etc the possible

discomfort for the player must be discounted. It is generally accepted that a substantial and abrupt increase in demands forces the organism to further adaptations, and therefore requires that the player should already have a successful performance profile.

Compared to a development in small steps longer periods of time are necessary to reach stability within an increased adaptive training situation. The possibilities of **progressive load increase are given through a change of the load components, through higher coordination training and through the number of competitions the player is required to play in.**

On a long-term basis, the changes of the load components are usually presented in the following order:
- Increased training frequency (training units per week),
- Increased training load within the training unit,
- Shortened breaks and increased training intensity.

Fig. 26: Pete Sampras in action on his favorite surface – grass.

THE PRINCIPLE OF DIVIDING INTO PERIODS AND CYCLES

An athlete cannot be in top-class competitive form all year long because he finds himself at the borderline of his particular capacity. This is dangerous, because the anabolic (= restorative metabolic process) total can change into a catabolic one i.e. dissimilation. For biological reasons a load change is necessary. The phase character of the course of adaptation with intensity, stabilization and reduction phase, demands long-term, after division of the training year into developing, stabilizing and reducing load periods (preparatory, competitive, transition period) and medium-term, in the frame of mesocycles, a change of load increasing, load containing and load-reducing micro cycles. Thereby on the one hand, overdemanding load can be avoided and on the other hand a higher peak of performance can be reached at certain times. More on this subject is shown in the chapters starting with 3.2.

THE ADDITIONAL PRINCIPLES INVOLVED IN TOP-CLASS TRAINING OF 14-25 YEAR OLDS

THE PRINCIPLE OF INDIVIDUALITY

For an optimal performance development, starting at approx. the age of 12-14, the personal situations of the players have to be given the coach's full attention. This in particular pertains to the various genetic components such as technical abilities, motor learning, plus physical make up, type of temperament, character, intellect, trainability, etc., in addition to more environmentally influenced components like motivation, resolution and others.

THE PRINCIPLE OF THE REGULATING INTERACTION BETWEEN INDIVIDUAL TRAINING ELEMENTS

What is discussed in this section here is the measured coordination of physical training and training technique. This is an important basis for the development to an individual top-class performance athlete, since different training elements can influence the outcome in a positive or negative manner. Physical training, in the area of top-class sports is to be seen mainly in relation to sport specific technique training. Therefore it also seems appropriate to consider **principles of technique training** during the planning of the type of loads to be applied and the implementation of fitness training. Experienced and successful trainers state ten basic and proven practical rules (cf. HOSSNER 1996, 84), of which two are commented on here:

THE PRINCIPLE OF COMPLEXITY

In the area of top sports a combined, complex sport specific training must be predominant, often with simultaneous technical, tactical and conditioning goals. The necessary performance requirements must be stimulated in such a way as to be very close to technique and in such manner that learned patterns of movement can be recalled under the highest demands of competition. This means that both coaches and players need a great deal of experience and intuitive feeling to successfully achieve this.

THE PRINCIPLE OF QUALITY AND PRECISION

Since top-class performance in tennis is combined with a very high quality of realization, players also have to get used to this precision pressure during training. This can be achieved, for example, through matches and training competition (for more cf. the following chapter 3.2).

THE PRINCIPLE OF CYCLIC REGENERATION

Assuming that performance control was optimally completed experience tells us that the high level performance life in tennis from the beginner to the top-class player lasts 8-15 years, If the players reach international level, this has to be grooved in through extreme training and competitive loads. It is therefore quite normal that after 2-6 years small performance losses occur, this despite an increased training. The causes of this situation are still not fully understood. Attempts to explain this problem, which relate to so-called "coordination barriers", "technique stagnations", over-straining of the different human systems (central nervous system, vegetative system, muscular system etc.) and stagnation, are but some of the reasons. Furthermore, next to these possible physiological causes, mental signs of fatigue (training and competitive weariness, no "bite") can also appear or be the actual cause.

A recipe used by many world-class athletes to overcome such a phase is to take time to regenerate. Olympic champions like Lasse VIREN (5.000 and 10.000 m), Alexander PUSCH (fencing), Rolf MILSER (weightlifting), many world-class tennis players like MCENROE, WILANDER etc. have all taken 6-12 month breaks from competition after producing top-class performances over 3-5 years and have severely reduced their training intensity, concentrating more on regenerating measures. In the time following, these athletes have again shown (and partially even increased) absolute top-class performance.

Further to this there will be an explanation put forward to cover in greater detail the individual steps involved in long-term performance development, and to this end the following will be covered
- General suggestions (and special aspects)
- Training goals and contents
- Training plan
- Tournament advice   Also: • Number of matches per year
                                      • Yearly plan

Fig. 27: Gustavo Kuerten is a further example of a South American performance explosion.

STEP 1: VERSATILE BASIC TRAINING
(APPROX: 4-6/7-YEAR-OLDS)
3.2

GENERAL REFERENCES

Children at this age achieve their first motor combinations that are predominately quantitative with less qualitative movement and with frequent unnecessary movements. They experience rapid increase in fast movements, speed and in terms of coordination as well as aerobic endurance. The leg muscles are well developed in contrast to those of the torso, the shoulder and arms. With regard to young children of this age it is not appropriate to use the term "training". Children should be given age-suitable and versatile motor training which has a very high level of play involved.

For this reason, the following motor forms are suggested as being appropriate:
• Motivated exercising
• Exercises that can be done individually or in small groups,
• where no large organizational measures are needed,
• that are inexpensive,
• which pose no great demand upon training equipment.

Regarding concentration, children of this age can't sustain long training sessions. For this reason the program has to change continuously, be diverse and encompass the whole body. It is very important to give the children a fair degree of choice in what they do and one cardinal rule is to accept the wishes and initiatives of the children!

TRAINING GOALS AND CONTENTS

• In any training regime for young children versatile general basic training with non-specific and varied ways of playing and complex motor forms around all body axes should take pride of place.
• The contents may be: children's gymnastics, judo, wrestling, ice-skating, different small ball games, throwing, catching etc. (see also Fig. 28).

- Within the specific area of tennis, a gradual and careful introduction for children to the technical basics of simple strokes with accompanying material should take place. In this context the term strokes does not mean stroke technique per se but rather the ball and racket control exercises including various coordination activities. The end if this period marks the possibility of slowly beginning with the introduction of actual tennis technique, through playing short and mini-tennis (more in "Advanced Techniques for Competitive Tennis", SCHÖNBORN, 1999).

Fig. 28: Judo is one of the ideal supplementary sports during childhood.

A PROPOSED TRAINING PLAN

The hours for exercising must be well planned: A regular training plan, however, does not exist at this age because fun, enjoyment and improvising should always be the main ingredients.

- The percentage portion of tennis-specific training should be no higher than 30% of the total exercising time. Basic training is of prime importance. Tennis or tennis-similar exercises are merely a part of the total program.

SUGGESTED BASIC TRAINING
- Training frequency per week: 2-3 times
- Training months per year: 5-7

That does not mean that exercising only takes place approx. a half-year, rather, the active months are spread over the whole year because of illness, vacation, organizational measures etc.

SUGGESTIONS FOR THE MAXIMUM NUMBER OF TOURNAMENTS
- If competition is organized, in whatever form according to the particular facilities, tennis should be only a part of the varied motor competitions (combined competition). The share of tennis in the final result also has to be judged as small.
- In addition, the rules have to be applied to the requirements and situations of the children.

STEP 2: BASIC TRAINING
(APPROX. 6/7-9/10-YEAR-OLDS)

3.3

GENERAL SUGGESTIONS

This age constitutes a phase of harmonious growth and physical differentiation in which above all, rapid progression in learning ability, in the development of coordination, reaction time and speed, of movement and aerobic capacity, are all seen. The ability to concentrate over a long period of time as well as performance directed motor abilities are as yet strictly limited.

Now, tennis specific training can begin. This does not mean that from now on, only, or to a major part, tennis is played! **Completely the opposite is true!** Again the term **'basic training'** points to the major content of this stage.

In this, as well as in the next phase of development (step 3), known as **the best motoric learning age**, the actual basics must be established for later,

Fig. 29: Patrick Rafter as a model athlete is the result of 15 years development training.

performance-oriented tennis. Therefore, continuing general training, with increasing intensity, exists in the foreground on the one side, and on the other side emphasis must be laid on the quality of stroke production. It is important that what is learned now doesn't have to be changed in a toilsome and time-consuming manner in the future. Having an eye on the quality of tennis techniques also means looking at running, jumping, throwing technique and other important motor processes, which are important to performance tennis.

TRAINING GOALS AND CONTENTS

Three main goals are paramount during this phase:
• The learning of basic tennis-specific techniques (on the basis of a favourable growth of the brain of approx. 90% of its mature size)
• Schooling of reaction and frequency speed (which are also dependent upon the central nervous system) and the
• Versatile training of the total motor system with main emphasis upon the coordination abilities (such as equilibrium, differentiating ability, rhythm etc.; see also Fig. 30).
• Training contents should relate to sport-specific technique in tennis, especially general and specific game and motor techniques, which train the perspective and anticipating abilities, as well as equilibrium, leg work, and the feel for the ball (see also Fig. 31).
• Please note! The schooling of tennis techniques is at this stage only one part of the total training!

A SUGGESTED TRAINING PLAN

• Training and tournament plans don't play a role at this stage yet.
• Training units, short and middle-term training goals should, however, be well prepared, especially special programs (such as technique and muscular development).
• Pure tennis training should encompass approximately 50% of the total training.
• Training frequency per week: 3-5 times.
• Training months per year: 6-8.

Fig. 30: Child as an all-rounder

Fig. 31: Handball is an additional ideal complementary sport where many important factors are schooled.

SUGGESTIONS FOR THE MAXIMUM NUMBER OF TOURNAMENTS

- In the beginning so-called mini-tennis tournaments should be played. Mini-tennis is the best form between the coordinative tennis specific pre-exercising; short tennis is vital in the process of learning the total court technique. Mini-tennis tournaments should not be overrated. It must be fun for the children to compete with an opponent, motivate them, give them the first tactical bases and strengthen their mental capabilities.

- The combined competitions, developed by R. SCHÖNBORN and introduced by the DTB (German Tennis Federation), have proved to be successful. Tennis however, still keeps playing a minor role (under 50% of total time). These competitions should also teach not only motor abilities, but also primarily team spirit.

- No tournaments with a Knock-Out system should be played at this age. When tennis tournaments are played in the final phase of this stage, then the type of tournament should guarantee the players several matches (box form, playing in two directions etc.). For children at this age, small club tournaments (between two ore more clubs) at the most, on a district basis are sufficient because the differences within these age groups are so minute that long trips to big or even international tournaments are senseless.

- No championships at this level: regional, national and even international championships should not take place at this age. Children should not be put under pressure to succeed or under stress. Competition should mean fun for them, without negative results.

- No ranking list: ranking list at this age can lead to premature pressure to succeed, to stress situations and they play no forecasting role regarding future careers. Their role can only be seen negatively.

- Sensible interpretation of tournament results: Tournament results should be used to check training results. They should, however, not be overrated, which can be very dangerous.

- During a tournament, stress situations with parents, officials and coaches must be absolutely avoided. The results should be seen down-to-earth and should always be judged positively. The player has to know that he is also allowed to lose.

- In the winter, for motivating reasons, approx. 2-4 tournaments.

- In the summer: 1-2 tournaments per month.

- Match training: to develop tactics, regular tactical training and match training is necessary.

SUGGESTED NUMBER OF MATCHES PER YEAR

At the most 30-40 matches at a local level: Not the number of tournaments is suggested but rather the number of matches. The purpose is, that tournaments are chosen according to the strength of the competitors, thus, allowing the player to play approx. 2-4 matches per tournament in order to give him a chance to have both positive and negative results.

It is not advisable to either under- or over-demand children during tournaments. Twenty tournaments with a defeat in the first round mean twenty matches played, but what a horrific result for the player.

STEP 3: DEVELOPMENT TRAINING (1) (APPROX. 9/10-11-/13-YEAR-OLDS)

3.4

GENERAL SUGGESTIONS AND SPECIAL ASPECTS

"This is the time of the best motor learning ability, the most harmonious growth and differentiating processes; rapid advancement is shown in inter-muscular coordination, reaction time, movement speed and also partially in speed strength. The maximum strength and anaerobic-lactic capacity are relatively weak"

(GROSSER/STARISCHKA [7]1998, 184).

This step is the first decisive stage for the later performance development. Mistakes that are made at this stage can hardly be corrected in the future. Now, a high quality in basic technique has to be strived for. Thereby the final technique is, as yet, not reached but a clear execution of the basic forms. Quality also dominates in other exercises (like throwing etc.).

All stroke techniques in their basic form have to be in place before the age of 12. Dependent upon age, slice, the topspin, drive, volley, smash, drop shot, two types of serves etc. should be used in a match. This means that in the second half of this stage the tennis specific elements slowly become more

Fig. 32: Serena Williams has, because of a tremendous and optimal development during her youth, the strongest strokes in women's tennis.

important. This does not mean that general training becomes less important. It only means that because of time constraints the training has to adapt to the specific demands of tennis. This means that more orientation in the direction of specific physical training for tennis has to be considered. Training of coordination as well as physical conditioning has to support and optimise tennis specific work of the trainee on the court.

Please note that the following examples are still unfortunately happening on the ground:
• Children who at this age play almost only tennis. As already mentioned, tennis technique development should be an important part at this stage, but it is only one part.
• Children playing too many tournaments. The tournament programme MUST be adapted to this age (see below).
• The orientation of the coach, parents and officials directed too strongly towards success rather than on harmonious development. Having success at this age is nice but unimportant and certainly doesn't show a direction for the future.

TRAINING GOALS AND CONTENTS
Since the brain and the central nervous system have now reached maturity and a harmonious growth situation exists, the following training goals are important:
• A qualitatively high standard technique training of all stroke and motor forms in tennis. Up to the 12th year of age, optimal learning of all techniques must have taken place.
• Next to the development of inter-muscular coordination, an eye also has to be put upon the intra-muscular coordination (i.e. the production of speed strength).
• The so-called time programmes, i.e. reaction time and speed of movement.
• In addition, through increasing technical perfection, training attention is now more orientated toward tactics.
• Training contents are therefore all exercises designed to avoid the previously mentioned problem areas, as well as additional exercises

designed to equalize and/or to avoid muscular imbalance. Certainly, considerable accent will still be put upon a general motor skills training.

CAUTION: On the basis of the given shortages in the maximal strength area (unstable skeletal system) and in the anaerobic-lactic energy availability, no overtaxing (e.g. long rallies) should take place.

PROPOSED TRAINING PLAN

- A training plan for the whole year, with detailed stages, monthly and weekly plans, will be carried out for the first time (otherwise there will be too much leeway for improvisation).
- Decisive for children within this load increase stage is the correct matching of training-regeneration-tournament-regeneration-training etc. The children have to gradually get used to such biological rhythms.
- Training frequency per week: 4-6 times
- Training months per year: 8-9

SUGGESTIONS FOR THE MAXIMUM NUMBER OF TOURNAMENTS

- At this age a sensible tournament plan should be set up, which in reality means a limited plan, because children should neither be overloaded nor confronted with difficult tournaments. Taking part in older categories should only be allowed where the child, performance wise has the possibility of a number of victories.

- Tournaments also promote tactical development: During tournament matches the tactical varieties from training should be tried out and tactical shortfalls that appear during tournament play should be worked upon when training.

- Tournaments should enhance motivation, which means children want to measure themselves through matches. Unending training de-motivates children from wanting to do further work.

- During match play, children learn to overcome the various stress factors, which means that during training such things as internal tension, environmental influence and the solving of external factors cannot be truly simulated. These can only be learned under actual tournament conditions.

- Tournament results should not be over-emphasized. It again has to be mentioned that results at this age play a secondary role in regard to a later career. Certainly, a child wants to win and should fight with all his might. A defeat should not be overly emphasized as a tragedy but has to be analysed sensibly and considered as a necessary and normal step in the future development.

RECOMMENDED NUMBER OF MATCHES PER YEAR

Approx. 40-50 matches, in addition double matches.

At this age doubles should be played regularly. In doubles, numerous details of technique are practiced, which are of great importance for modern singles tennis, for example, the short cross return from both sides and with both kinds of strokes (forehand, backhand), first volley near the T-line through direction reduction etc.

Yearly Plan For Training And Tournaments

Month	Period/Training	Tournaments
October	T.P.	None
November	T.P.	None
December	P.P.1	None
January	P.P.2	1-2
February	C.P.	3-4
March	C.P. and T.P.	2-3
April	T.P. and P.P.1	None
May	P.P.2	1-2
June	C.P.	2-3
July	C.P.	2-3
August	C.P.	2-3
September	C.P. and T.P.	1-2/none

Explanation of the descriptions
P.P.1: First part of the preparatory period, in which the development of all factors takes place
P.P.2: Second part of the preparatory period in which tactics, match training and the complex, match-oriented realisation of trained elements should take place.
C.P.: Competition period in which next to training, taking part in tournaments is most important.
T.P.: Transition period needed for rest, recuperation and general regeneration.

Based on decades of experience the above suggested yearly plan is certainly not set in tablets of stone, but should be seen as a possible model. As mentioned, development and training of most factors has to be continued during the period of competition.

What has to be adhered to are the individual preparatory periods, **without taking part in tournaments**. Because so many areas are not sufficiently stabilized, young players and their coaches should, at least once a year, have a sufficient long time to build, improve, stabilize or even change, with restrictions eventually resulting (loss of form, performance decrease). Additionally, it would be an advantage if approximately twice a year a shorter period of time is available for the same purpose. These preparatory periods automatically change within the next phases and the tournament periods become longer, therefore leaving less time available for necessary changes or adjustments.

The major points of the individual periods as well as the necessary regenerating phases without tennis must be adhered to.

Fig. 33: Martina Hingis has an excellent tennis technique, feel for the ball and is tactically the top woman player in world tennis.

3.5
STEP 4: DEVELOPMENT TRAINING (2) (APPROX. 11-/13-14/15-YEAR-OLDS)

GENERAL SUGGESTIONS AND SPECIAL ASPECTS

It was stated during the previous step that it was the first decisive leg, so this next step is the first critical one in the development of a young tennis player. Through the start of the first puberty phase and the following physical and mental changes (accelerated growth, sex diverging hormonal changes, restructuring motoric abilities and skills, reduced motoric learning ability etc.) it can lead to setbacks, temporary stagnations, to mental and physical as also to other personal problems.

It is however important to remember that this is not inevitable. By all means, this age is a challenge for every coach because he is confronted, as a rule, for the first time with opposition, contradiction, disciplinary problems, desire to be independent, knowing better etc. the start of hormonal change can lead to gender specific differences as well as to development differences in respect to acceleration and retardation. Thereby on the one hand, performance leaps occur, on the other hand stagnation is possible.

Caution is urged when dealing with successful girls:
They are pressed too fast toward an almost 100% entry into adult and WTA tennis. It is hoped that on the basis of explanations in this book, the great danger of a too rapid entry into professional tennis has been made clear.

It is without question that a combination between the own age category, the older category and partially adult tennis, is to be suggested for very successful girls.

One just has to know where and how the higher tournament load can be justifiable and above all, beneficial. Here, sensibility and experience is asked on the part of the coaches. Much can be destroyed, that has previously shown to be developing well.

TRAINING GOALS AND CONTENTS

In spite of the above problems, not only do previously developed abilities and skills have to be further intensified but also new contents have to be taken up, such as the start of a purposeful muscle development and the promotion of aerobic capacity.

• In the second phase of this step, speed strength and endurance training has to be intensified and a correct training system must be introduced in this area of work. In other words: increased force development training (general and specific) as well as a balancing of possible muscular imbalance (as a result of increased training matches and participation in tournaments).

• Speed develops more slowly, meaning, on the basis of the described problems, difficulties in the area of speed should be expected. This does not mean that training of these factors should be neglected. The opposite is true. More importantly now seems to be the optimal development for the previous steps. Time programs, frequency speed, action speed, reaction speed and speed strength (velocity ability) have to find further emphasis in the training plan.

In the area of technique:
• If technique is systematically developed in the previous steps, all techniques should be available in relative high quality. Now it is necessary to continue to perfect the player's potential and above all, to bind together the coordination and conditioned elements, as well as to further increase the complexity in training (e.g. also SCHÖNBORN 1999).
• The application in situ and the chances to achieve success should be increased.
• Tactics training becomes more important through the perfection of technique. At this stage the individual's conduct should be reviewed.
• At this level, differences have to be made between the sexes.
Girls mature faster. Accelerated physical and mental development leads to advantages in the adaptation to training stimuli, whereby technique and conditioning development increases. An eventual increase in weight, through a higher share of fat, slows down this developmental advantage.

Therefore more attention must be put upon the nutrition in girls and young women. Male adolescents are normally 1-2 years biologically behind girls.

SUGGESTED TRAINING PLAN

- The yearly training plan and its cyclical subdivisions should now be more closely scrutinized. Without detailed planning, up to and including stringent training units, no optimal performance control will be possible.

- Because loads and demands continually increase in training, above all, through a longer tournament season, it is especially important to scrutinize the rest and regeneration processes and measures more closely.

- Training frequency per week: 4-8 times.

- Approximately two training units per day are necessary at the end of this step because the extent and contents rise and show more variety, so that the regenerating phase would not be sufficient in one training unit. If both phases can be completed in half a day, or if both daily halves are necessary depends upon the player's time and/or upon training contents.

- Months of training per year: 8-10.

SUGGESTED MAXIMUM NUMBER OF TOURNAMENTS

- Tournaments, in this phase, should still be seen as feedback required to control performance. No pressure to succeed should be exerted. Tournaments should confirm the correctness of training methods, contents, extents, intensities etc. and/or give reasons for change.

- Tournament quality is determined through the one-third principle; that means the players should basically play 1/3 of all matches against weak opponents, 1/3 against equal opponents and 1/3 against strong opponents. Against weaker opponents they have to prove they can hold these players at a distance. Hereby they learn to defend their position, to overcome the fear of failure, not to underestimate their opponent and to develop self-confidence. Against equal opponents they have to learn how to fight, to overcome the fact of being behind in points, to never give up, to accept a change in form, to change unsuccessful tactics and unsatisfactory external conditions etc. Against strong opponents they can play freely and openly, grow beyond their ability, discover unknown performance abilities, new tactics or may even apply new strokes, stroke speed or new stroke variations. This one-third principle (two victories and then a possible defeat) makes it possible for the player to get into the top 20 ranking in world professional tennis.

• At the end of this step, junior girls can begin a careful entry into women's tennis: approximately 1/3 of all tournaments can either be played in older categories or women's categories, approx. 2/3 in one's own category.

• Participation of juniors in men's tennis remains an exception, they can, however, participate according to playing ability in the older youth categories.

• The strongest junior boys and girls can individually take part in international tournaments and team competition, because at this age the youth should get used to the mental pressure which exists in international tournaments and also become acquainted with other opponents, ways of playing and other styles. Team competition is of main importance for the development of team spirit.

• The combination between youth tournaments in one's own and in a higher category or in the adult category has to be carried out very carefully on an individual basis. As mentioned previously, participation in a higher class of play (especially international) tournaments and/or by adults, depends upon playing strength, physical and mental development position, the perspectives, the goals set and the economic and organizational possibilities. As such a general recommendation cannot be given.

• Generally it is important to reiterate the fact, that match experience can only be achieved by playing matches. If the tournament levels are set too high, however, neither a winning attitude nor a feeling of self-confidence will appear. Furthermore, the player will not gain positive match experience, other than if he plays tournaments continuously (thereby giving up a sensible training development) which unfortunately is still often the case, finally leading to the above described negative experiences.

Also tactics which are schooled in training, reach a necessary high grade quality only through tournaments.

SUGGESTED NUMBER OF MATCHES PER YEAR
Approx. 60 matches in addition to double matches.

Yearly Plan For Training And Tournaments

Month	Period/Training	Tournaments
October	T.P.	None
November	P.P.1/T.P	None
December	P.P.1/2	(2)
January	P.P.2 and C.P..	2-3
February	C.P.	2-3
March	C.P. and T.P..	2
April	T.P. and P.P.1	None
May	P.P.2	2
June	C.P.	2-3
July	C.P.	3-4
August	C.P.	2-3
September	C.P. and T.P.	1-2

Fig. 34: The unique performance of Pete Sampras is a result of a perfect technique, excellent speed and optimal strength.

STEP 5: CONNECTING TRAINING
(APPROX. 14/15-16-/18-YEAR-OLDS)

3.6

GENERAL SUGGESTIONS

This step is the second decisive leg for the future performance development in tennis, and perhaps the most important one of all. Because it is so decisive it has to be completed very successfully. Responsible for this are not only the age level implementing professionally correct training contents, but also the already described systematic long-term development in previous steps which has to be seen as a prerequisite! The adolescent, as seen from the point of view of his development, can, on the basis of his gradual pubertal growth, undertake even heavier training loads. All areas can already be included in the training.

This step is also decisive for the development of the player's individuality, for the perfection of the tactical abilities and for the moral attitudes during a match. For this reason, a strongly increased participation in tournaments is necessary and for the first time, the tournament results play an important role. If up to now, tournament results and positions in the ranking list only served as a form of feedback providing training control which had little meaning from the players perspective, success in tournaments now presents a certain criteria and prerequisite for a successful career. The player now has to be able to successfully apply his long-term achievements in a match.

The perfecting of the situational technique must be completed and training must be oriented towards the individual needs of each player. This is why group training at the end of this step is only to be suggested in exceptional cases and only by certain aspects of training.

Fitness training, coordination training, technique and tactical training have to be individually planned and individual strengths and weaknesses have to be considered! Each successful player is his own person. Whoever misses decisive points at this step, has only in exceptional cases the chance of reaching the peak in tennis. An analysis, gathered in the last decades, of players from throughout the world, confirms this point.

Nevertheless, the above mentioned facts are only suggestions and are not a guarantee of success at the top. To reach this goal, very much has to be done and done correctly at the next stage in the following years.

With regard to junior girls, the change into women's tennis is now taking place. Further performance demands have to be achieved by juniors, in order to make the step into adult tennis possible at a later period.

Between the 15th and 17th year of age, most successful girls have a tendency to want to change over to the professional tennis. The problem that exists, however, is that while most junior girls have the playing ability to compete professionally but cannot cope with the physical and mental demands of the professional tour. That is why so many give up. The few exceptions of very successful junior girls cannot be seen as a criterion! These are simply exceptions. A long-term sensible growth toward professional tennis is certainly the far more successful and also healthier path. We have discussed the "burn-out" and "drop-out" features at the beginning (cf. p. 13). Again, sensible performance control is the key against such syndromes.

CONFLICT BETWEEN TENNIS AND FULL TIME EDUCATION

The successful and competitive adolescent has to play tournaments and even tournament series, which leads to repeated absence from school. Not all schools or teachers accept this. Thereby the young player falls further and further behind in his schoolwork and has an increasingly harder time catching up. Many years' experience on the part of one of the authors in the Federal Performance Center (BLZ) of the German Tennis Federation (DTB) shows that a common sense settlement with the school is necessary. Beyond that, private lessons have to be organized, which again has to be arranged with the school.

Most school directors and teachers are willing to agree upon a reasonable settlement. One should never make maximum demands, no school would agree upon that. Leave the school with or without a junior high school diploma and only play tennis? One of the authors has, in his active 26-year period as head coach of the German Tennis Federation, never once suggested a premature discontinuance of school. As long as one can agree upon going to school and to training but above all going to tournaments, the students should not leave school! With a calculation of 3-5 hours daily training and approx. 9 hours sleep, then a difference of approx. 10-12 hours remains for school, homework, personal chores and eventually free time.

This attitude demands extreme self-discipline, punctuality, and toughness and doing ones duty, all attributes he later needs daily, as a possible top player. If the players quota of success rises rapidly and he has to follow tournament commitments over a longer period of time he can still decide if he wants to leave school. Then he has a real perspective of his professional career as a player and knows which risks he can afford.

TRAINING GOALS AND CONTENTS
- This is the ideal age to optimise all techniques up to the level of virtuosity
  - Goal oriented training with the goal of situational perfection, the ability to solve difficult situations, ability to achieve success through one's own technique and a continuing increase of stroke and game velocity are the major importance (see SCHÖNBORN 1999).
  - The goal should be reached at the end of this phase, the basis having been laid in the previous phases.

- Competitive training as an important point of emphasis: we thereby mean match-like training, where technique and tactically difficult situations have to be mastered. The pressure to play winners calls for partial aggressiveness and a stringent capability to prevail. This should be trained regularly and not just during tournaments. One can only successfully apply in a tournament what has been trained with success thousands of times and thereby stored in one's memory.

- Closely combined with it is also the so-called "anti-stress training" as a further point of emphasis. Typical stress situations during a match can hardly be imitated during training; nevertheless, one should provoke stress situations through increasingly difficult training requirements (training during strong winds with poor or different balls, with noise, on different playing surfaces during a training unit, after a hard fitness training with a strong load). This should not happen too much because of the danger of over-taxing.

- Increased muscle development and force training: now biologically positive premises for muscle development training (hypertrophy) are given. The muscles also have to be made to contract rapidly for accelerating purposes (start off, strokes, etc.); that means a strengthened reactive and force training has to be implemented.

- Next to the aerobic metabolism, the anaerobic lactic metabolism has to be improved. Although the tennis player is relative rarely over acidified and when, not to a high degree, the lactate tolerance should also be trained. The biological provisions are given at this age.

SUGGESTED TRAINING PLAN

- A beginning period of approx. 6-7 weeks should start by the beginning of October or November, of course this phase can be planned somewhat earlier or later but should not be shortened for new developments, because sufficient adaptation times must be guaranteed. Besides, at this age there are a number of things to optimise, for which at a later period no more time will be available.
- A similar developing phase is planned for March/April but, by experience, only 3-4 weeks are available. During such a short period of time there is little chance for big changes or improvements to be made. All the more time during tournaments has to then serve for further training.
- Because tournament time is now divided into so-called blocks, special value has to be put upon sufficient regeneration. One should not forget that youths are not as yet fully loadable. The waste of energy is much higher than with experienced adults, especially when the young players play successfully. Therefore, much more time must be given to the period of regeneration. Here the motto is: less is more!
- Training frequency per week: 6-12 times
- Training months per year: 9-10

TOURNAMENT SUGGESTIONS

- Increasing tournament participation:
  At this age, gradually more frequent tournament success should appear. The time of predominant performance development control is over, the player now has to show that he can also successfully make use of the training potential in tournaments. For that reason it is important that he is not "burned out" through wrong and exaggerated tournament planning. A gradually sensible tournament planning with realistic goals and achievable success outlooks, with a slowly increasing difficulty grade is to be recommended. The present day practice of the normal, thoughtless chase after ranking points throughout the world, cost what it may, leads sooner or later to increasing unsuccessfulness and frustration. In order to act correctly, the individuality of the player has priority. That is why team development is questionable. The advantage for one player can mean a great disadvantage for another player. Individual, professionally competent coaching is the by far better alternative. Up to small exceptions that, however, are always quoted as a reason to recommend such projects. Most "team projects" have failed sooner or later. There is certainly no reason, however, to oppose the building of loose teams of player and coaches for a short period of time, for example, to play a few tournaments. But also within these teams each player has to be cared for individually.

- At the end of this step, the junior players begin to play in higher categories or with the men. A division is suggested in which approx. 1/3 of all tournaments are played in the highest junior class, or, depending upon playing strength, with the adults, and 2/3 are played under 16. Especially successful juniors can more often take part in international youth competitions (playing singles or in teams).

- By junior girls the tendency exists to change into women's tennis, that is why the division here looks somewhat different.

- A division is suggested, in which approx 1/3 of tournaments are played in their own category, and 2/3 of all tournaments in the highest category or with the adult women.

- For both sexes, exceptions are the rule:
  Especially talented and strong playing adolescents who are far ahead of their age group should begin earlier (with women almost completely) with adult competition, but only under the condition that they hardly have equal opponents within junior competition and already play successfully with the adults. The premature participation of an immature player with the active players under the premise of wanting to collect experience or to get a few early points in the world ranking lists, as a rule, has a negative effect. This effect will increase through a continuous lack of success, frustration, fear of failure, loss of self-esteem and respectability and finally, results in a "burn-out" and possibly "drop-out".

SUGGESTED NUMBER OF MATCHES PER YEAR

Approx. 70 matches in addition to double matches.

Yearly Plan For Training And Tournaments

Month	Period/Training	Tournaments
October	T.P. or P.P.1	None
November	P.P.1	(1-2)
December	P.P.1 + P.P.2	1-2
January	C.P.	3-4
February	C.P.	3-4
March	C.P. and T.P.	1-2
April	T.P. and P.P.1+2	1
May	C.P.	3-4
June	C.P.	3-4
July	C.P. (T.P.)	3-4 (1-2)
August	C.P.	3-4
September	C.P. and T.P.	1-2

An organization of tournament participation in tournament blocks is suggested, where, according to success and/or effort, 3-4 tournaments are played in a row, followed by a regeneration period, with a following training period in which certain faults that occurred are improved and/or new elements are trained.

Fig. 35: André Agassi has again reached the absolute peak of world tennis through strength training.

STEP 6: TOP-CLASS TRAINING
(FROM APPROX. 16/19 YEARS OF AGE)
3.7

GENERAL REFERENCES

Biologically speaking the physical maturity of adults is reached by the age of 16 to 19 years. Now, the last step of development in tennis begins, lasting until the end of the active career. Work geared specifically at a certain individual and the stabilization of the individual player's skills and tactics should reach their peak. At the latest, beginning with this step, which should be completed by the time the player reaches 25-26 years of age, the perfect foundation for the top-performance building should be completed with the player and standing very securely.

In the precious steps hard work on a systematic, long-term basis was put into the foundation construction. At this stage the achieved "perfection" is turned into virtuosity. In comparison to the previous steps Top-class training differs in a number of areas. Not only the already discussed individuality of each player is reflected in the training process, two additional important aspects must be considered as well:

1. The enormous increase in tournament participation excludes longer training periods, if we like it or not, even if it contradicts the theoretical laws of the science of training. We have to look at reality. That is why the whole training system will be changed and adapted to the tournament season. That means training and development training must be continued during the tournaments. That demands a transformation of the normal theories of training and a tremendous knowledge of the coaches involved.

2. Through the previous long-term training and developing period, the organism has adapted itself to many areas and has thereby become immune toward training stimuli, which was actually the training goal. Through repetition of previous loads, ranges, intensities, training forms etc., no additional adaptation processes will be brought about and

therefore no additional performance increase will be achieved. New ways have to be found to make another increase in performance possible. These paths are getting shorter because of physiological reasons. That is why they have to be changed more often. That also demands a high level of knowledge from the participating coaches!

The player must be controlled more carefully, more sensitively and more precisely, the more his performance increases. At this level of performance the air is rather thin. The inability to bring about continuous new and sensible changes in training is the worldwide main reason for long-term stagnation between the approx. ages of 20-25 of a large number of talented players.

SPECIAL ASPECTS
- **The change from junior into senior tennis:**
  The importance of managing this change is mostly underestimated. Many think that eventual success during the youth period can be automatically continued at the adult level. However, there is a great difference between junior and senior tennis. Not only that the unknown ranking number 300 can play very good tennis but also experience is missing which has nothing to do with the opponent, but rather with the whole atmosphere, the changed circumstances, the enormous performance pressure, long trips, being suddenly alone, having no training partners etc. All this has to be internalised and the new situation has to be accepted. Additional essentials appear: One has to understand the pressure, cleverness, routine, and variation in tennis involved in playing a new opponent and to slowly find the answer.

- **The hard path through the qualification:**
  Today, every qualification is an independent strong tournament. One needs three to five victories in order to qualify for the main field. Then one usually plays against a seeded player in the first round. This situation not only demands a perfect condition but also mental strength and enormous resistance and strength of will, especially when one is defeated in the first round.

- **Problems with private coaches:**
  On the one hand the player needs a good coach, that he probably can't afford to pay, not considering that there are hundreds of new players per year but only a few very good tour coaches available world-wide and they are practically always booked out. For this reason young players, in desperation, usually engage inexperienced and inexpensive coaches who usually present more of a load than help. As long as national associations or sponsors don't give them support, major problems will appear in this area.

- **Financial problems of the tour:**
  No big money is earned in the qualifying rounds and so the whole business starts off on a negative basis. If no sponsors are available the start of a career can be financially very tough in the beginning, because flights, hotels and food cost a good deal of money, especially when one considers that there are 20-25 tournaments per year world-wide.

TRAINING GOALS AND CONTENTS

- Increased attention on such as individual needs and the stabilization of different areas of technique and skill.
  From here on the young player/star has to play "big" tennis, with the goal of climbing up the ranking list as fast as possible. Statistics of the world stars show that those who have reached the top 10 of the ATP needed, from the start of their professional tennis career, up to the top 100 an average of 15 months, and from there into the top 10 an average of 19.7 months. That makes only two years and ten months from 0 into the top 10 and that, practically, without exceptions. That means only a well-prepared player can take such a leap.

- Training encompasses the total spectrum of technique, condition, tactics, psyche etc. It is self-evident that in top-class training not only individual strengths are continuously improved and still existing weakness diminished, but in the sense of further changes to different techniques also new training contents must be tried out. Additionally players have to be pushed more often to the limit of their capacity. Coaches, therefore, need a higher theoretical and practical knowledge. Through improvising and/or continuing what has always been done, no further development is possible. At this point, many young talented players fail.

- Match-simulated training and quality have absolute priority.
  If one accepts the fact that the basis of a flawless technique is given and that the conditioning situation has reached its demanded peak, further development can only be reached through the quality and the correct contents of training. Here it is important to note: quality before quantity on the one hand, and an expansion of action ability on the other side. *"Through virtuosity and perfecting the specific application, the action competence of the player should be enlarged"* (SCHÖNBORN 1999). That means concentration must be applied, above all, during the training of existing action problems, action weakness, and the lack of specific prerequisites. Possibly responsible for the eventual lack of action prerequisites may be coordination, conditioning, technique, and tactical or mental areas.

A SUGGESTED TRAINING PLAN

At this step it is suggested that no further orientation plans are put into effect, they should be individually developed. The player should organize his tournament program according to his playing class and ranking position.

The result is a first possible training plan. This plan should contain training periods of at least 3-4 weeks duration, held at least twice a year and contain a minimum of three to four longer regeneration periods.

Rushing from tournament to tournament without regeneration and basic systematic training may partially present a certain number of successful results (match experience) but in the long run, it means a slow decline in substance and a reduction in performance ability.

TOURNAMENT SUGGESTIONS

During adolescence top junior players should take part in, at the most, grand slam youth tournaments and eventually concentrate upon World and European Championships. The actual goal, however, is to play with the professionals. Juniors who have not yet positioned themselves in the front rankings, should according to their schedule, take part in numerous youth competitions in order to gather more playing experience. Finally, the player's goal is to achieve a sensible individual combination between youth and adult competition.

MATCH NUMBER PER YEAR

Approximately 70-80 matches in addition to double matches.

Fig. 36 gives a summary of the long-term performance development in tennis.

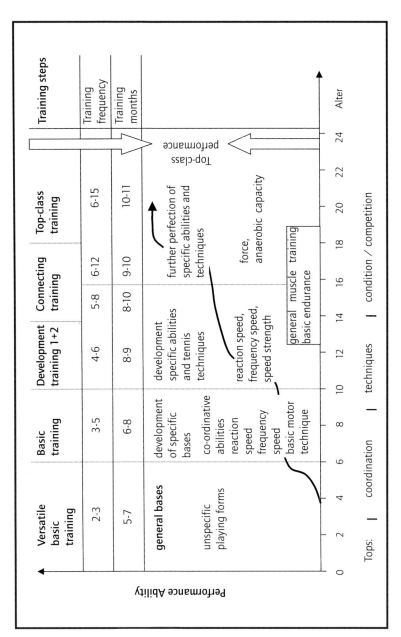

Fig. 36: The long-term performance development in tennis (from: GROSSER/STARISCHKA '1998, 185)

Fig. 37: Nicolas Kiefer is an example of strong playing and mental individuality, with all the accompanying advantages and disadvantages present in a different form among all world-class players.

4 PROBLEMS WITH TALENT IN TENNIS

4.1 WHAT IS TALENT?

Talent can mean different things to different people, but within the terms of reference of this book it is taken to mean as follows.

Young people who in relation to others of their own age, show above-average abilities and/or performance, are described as having talent. They appear to have more genetic traits that together with environmental influences can develop into high quality performance. It has not as yet been possible to convincingly quantify the share of talent in a specific individual.

Talent dependent performance determining abilities and skills, for the sport of tennis, relate to general and specific coordination skills, plus learning related, psychic, mental and individual areas. A prognosis of talented players should always be given with utmost care because only through the course of the years can concrete answers be given regarding great possibility of future success. Possible talent should be identified and after many years of promotion (i.e. performance control) real talent may be recognized.

4.2 TALENT IDENTIFICATION

The present practice in the sport of tennis is, in general, to look at tournament results and ranking lists of children under the motto:

The successful ones and those with the highest ranking must have the most talent!

This is the greatest mistake that can be made. Many names of the last thirty years can be listed as negative examples, who were all victims of ignorance and over-ambition (parents!).

The following are two positive examples of later top-class players from Germany – Boris Becker and Michael Stich. Both were not the no.1 or 2 in their age class. Boris Becker never won the German Youth Championships until reaching the age of 15. He was under the best five or six of his age group between the ages of 10 and 15, tending more toward the lower half of the group, however. When he was 15, he became German Youth Champion for the first time. Three times he took part in the European Youth Championships, which he never won and where he only reached the semi-finals once!

Up to the age of thirteen Michael Stich was a better soccer than tennis player. He entered DTB promotion rather late and won the German Youth Championships for the first time with 18. He successfully completed secondary school, and not until then (when 19 years of age) did he start with professional tennis.

Both were not the most successful young stars but later won Wimbledon, the Davis Cup and much more! Both have one thing in common. In their youth they were differently but systematically built up in all motor and mental areas and over a period of many years. One of the authors of this book was a witness of this development because he was also responsible for youth promotion in the German Tennis Federation (DTB) and worked mainly with these players within the DTB. Other German players like e.g. Ch. STEEB, E. JELEN, P. KÜHNEN, U. RIGLEWSKI, or S. HANIKA, B. BUNGE, Cl. KOHDE, E. PFAFF, I. CUETO, S. HACK went, with many others, more or less along the same developmental path- at the same time, and later became very successful in men's and women's tennis. Only Steffi Graf as an absolute exceptional talent "marched" (starting with 12 years) with great success through all age categories.

HOW DOES TALENT IDENTIFICATION WORK?

If one wants to discover talent, one has to lean upon many details and situations and not only upon tournament results and a one-time playing exhibition (regarding the technique situation). Especially these last two aspects are the reason why so many highly praised private projects and groups have failed, without exceptions, in the course of the last decades, up to today and will continue to do so.

If the path is correct, then with the help of practical and possibly also sport scientific analysis processes, to analyse the general motoric athletics-specific talent components and set up careful prognoses. Talent identification does not mean seeing the future champion in a child.

These mistakes could, among others, lead to the consequence that by sighting talents, one concentrates on too few (and possibly not the right) talents. A larger number of sighted players is always better, because the greater is the chance to find real talents later.

STEPS IN TALENT IDENTIFICATION

1. Within a group of 6-12-year-old children it is important to recognize basic abilities based on experience and observance. These may include that the ability to "move" with more agility and in a playful manner is better developed in these youngsters than in other group members. This is considered a rough "negative selection".

2. **After 3-6 weeks,** motor tests are administered for general coordination and conditioning.

3. **After an additional 2-6 months,** sport scientific investigation processes should be used in the following way:
   • Biomechanical processes to calculate time programs, reactive strength and speed strength.
   • Performance physiological processes to determine the aerobic/ anaerobic capacities.

4. Parallel to the second and third steps (above), it is necessary by means of a **checklist** (cf. SCHÖNBORN 1992) to carry through a complex, subjective-objective listing of dates and talents. These dates support on the one hand, sport-specific selection on the other hand, and a special recognition of psychic/mental components. This latter area plays a decisive role in performance tennis; ambition, will, hardness, diligence, self-confidence, ability to withstand stress, braveness, fighting spirit, self-discipline and many more indispensable prerequisites of a future top-

class player. Of course, this whole field cannot be tested quickly; one needs a long period of time because a number of qualities mentioned can still be taught during the promotion period.

References to the check-list (cf. table 6).
In this section the individual important prerequisites of a future international champion are gathered. Next to the ever more important bodily structure, which comprises the body height (average size of the top 10 with men is presently 188,5 cm and with women 175,7 cm, tendency rising), muscular requirements (predominant fast muscle fibres), muscle mass and muscular division (preferred are leptosomic types) as well as the relationship of extremities and torso (rather longer extremities and normal torso). Further the motoric (2-5), the tennis specific (6-9), the so important receptive and transferable (10-11) and the mental area (12-24) is listed. The importance of this last area is shown through the high number of points.

Also the section pertaining to surroundings is of great importance. The quality and the commitment of the clubs, the federation and the coaches, the common sense of the parents, the positive attitude and support of the school as well as the positive influence of friends within and outside of sports strongly influence the athletic development and above all the speed of them. Studies make clear that the driving distance to the place of training and to school plays a decisive role. The major number of national champions, world champions, Olympic champions and champions of big international competitions in all possible sports had, according to these tests, very short distances, in their youth, between their home, school and training area. The top German tennis players of the 80s and 90s also confirmed this fact. Long drives mean an enormous loss in time, stress, fatigue and finally a drop in motivation.

How to use the check list?
In the evaluation scale are, next to the question marks, five evaluation criteria: -- very poor, - poor, 0 average, + good, ++ very good.

If one starts with a newcomer one doesn't know much about him. In this case one circles the question mark in the appropriate line, at least so long until one has reached the first objective judgement. Normally many question

Personal data

Name:	Date of birth:
	Place of birth:
Training age:	Day of first analysis:
Coach:	Day of last analysis:

Person specific abilities:	very poor
1. body build	++ + 0 − −− ?
2. coordination	++ + 0 − −− ?
3. speed	++ + 0 − −− ?
4. endurance	++ + 0 − −− ?
5. strength	++ + 0 − −− ?
6. leg work	++ + 0 − −− ?
7. technique	++ + 0 − −− ?
8. tactics	++ + 0 − −− ?
9. play-wit	++ + 0 − −− ?
10. speed of learning	++ + 0 − −− ?
11. speed of performance	++ + 0 − −− ?
12. ambition	++ + 0 − −− ?
13. will power	++ + 0 − −− ?
14. mental toughness	++ + 0 − −− ?
15. diligence in applying training methods	++ + 0 − −− ?
16. self-confidence	++ + 0 − −− ?
17. hope for success	++ + 0 − −− ?
18. stress resistance	++ + 0 − −− ?
19. bravery	++ + 0 − −− ?
20. fighting spirit	++ + 0 − −− ?
21. ability to anticipate	++ + 0 − −− ?
22. ability to concentrate	++ + 0 − −− ?
23. self-discipline	++ + 0 − −− ?
24. good behavior on and off court	++ + 0 − −− ?

Environmental specific abilities:	
1. club	++ + 0 − −− ?
2. federation	++ + 0 − −− ?
3. coach	++ + 0 − −− ?
4. parents	++ + 0 − −− ?
5. school	++ + 0 − −− ?
6. friends	++ + 0 − −− ?
7. distance to reach training venue	++ + 0 − −− ?

Table 6: Talent check-list (note SCHÖNBORN 1992)

marks are circled in the beginning. Where an objective judgement has already been reached, a circle is made around the appropriate evaluation sign.

Now one starts the training session with the player. One wins more and more impressions and knowledge about the player and can change the scale, complement it or make it more precise. After a certain period of time one gets a relatively objective actual standing. Now one can, on the basis of these actual facts, work systematically on weaknesses and strengths. During the course of time, the individual evaluations (better, has gotten worse, remained the same) will become more precise, change and stabilize. After two years one should have a very precise, objective picture of the protégé in order to eventually give a correct prognosis for the future. This check-list does not of course present uniform criteria for all coaches and players. The evaluation scale has to fit into realistic goals. A club coach will have other values in front of him than for example a federal coach, who has to keep an eye on the world's top players. A certain amount of experience, however, is necessary in order to be successful.

4.3 ——————————— TALENT DEVELOPMENT

Through reading the information above it is possible to see that talent spotting should not be a short-term or even one-time process. In fact just the opposite is true, this is a long-term process that can, under certain circumstances, last a number of years. The final goal of talent spotting is the "talent selection success", which means, the smaller the percentage of those selected, the higher the percentage of the successfully selected.

For financial and other reasons it is not sensible to promote and pull along a big group of less talented or untalented youths. At some stage in the future someone will have to make a decision on behalf of only a few, and the better and more conscientiously the pre-selection took place, the more success will be achieved with the selection and promotion, with a smaller risk, that suitable talents will drop away.

IMPORTANT POINTS FOR TALENT DEVELOPMENT

• First of all, **optimal development and training conditions** have to be created for those considered as and eventually identified as talented. This is still a big problem in today's tennis.

• To carry out training correctly and to realize and reach presented goals it is necessary to have an **excellent organization, and a high quality on work.**
Therefore, coaches have to guarantee that they have an extensive, in depth **professional knowledge** in all relevant areas of the science of sports, but also the financial and organizational responsibilities required on behalf of parents and additionally local officials have to be guaranteed. With few exceptions, these are still the main weak spots in tennis.

• It is advantageous that **at an early age children and adolescents** should receive common training in small groups. Such groups give children support, they can cheer them up, youths can learn from the suggestions of their training partners and the natural comparison of strength and organized playful competition motivates and accelerates their learning process. Beyond this, individual breaks (when changing during an exercise) can lead to a form of natural regeneration. Because the development of almost all healthy children up to the age of 11/12 years is similar, no great differences in the load and content are necessary to ensure quality training, similar age groups should be relatively homogenous and therefore both sexes can train together without problems. That changes, are however, more and more, with the progression of biological maturity and the development of playing and performance strength.

- How a **consequent and correct promotion over a number of years** can be organized was explained in detail in chapter 3. At this stage, we would merely like to point out several complementary (also repeating) aspects, which relate especially to still existing faults in talent development.

- Unfortunately, still too little value is put upon individual promotion up to the age of the middle adolescent period (13/15).
  - Through decades of experience the following 11-/12-13-/14-year-old adolescents can, on a common basis, train 50-60% of their training content; within 40-50% of the training period, individual necessities and problems should be of primary importance. That means, at this age, half of the training period is used to set individual focal points, which can of course also be trained in a group.
  - With the age of 13/14 years, more individual attention and training with special individual focusing dominates.

  That demands, next to professional knowledge, optimal training organization and individual planning. Daily improvisation is no satisfying method of control.

- It is also to be observed, that training contents, methods and intensities etc. remain the same during the total youth and adolescent period, and

- that development success is mistakenly measured solely through competition results.

- An additional mistake is that starting with childhood, too many people want to simultaneously influence the individual; parents, several coaches, officials at various levels, promoters and sponsors want to of course do "the best" for their protégé, prevent, however, through different individual interests and to a large degree through lacking professional knowledge, a harmonious and detailed plan of development. One sole professional expert (a coach!) must decide, coordinate, plan and carry the responsibility. Of course he can and should have several co-workers (good team work) but he alone makes the decisions. During childhood and adolescence, three top trainers at the most should successively train the talents. Parents should as much as possible (at best, fully) keep out of daily training. Up to a few exceptions, which were also no solution for a longer period of time and ended mostly with a big bang, serious early (at the latest within the first puberty phase) confrontations started between parents and children, with partially disastrous consequences for their future development. The parents of Boris Becker, for example, who from the beginning kept clear of the practical promotion and care of their son, demonstrated an ideal attitude.

- Unfortunately non-existing training concepts and plans are the rule. Without professional planning, the wide spectrum of performance limiting and performance increasing factors cannot be overlooked or accomplished. Only systematic weekly training work can guarantee success! The numerously explained developmental complexity cannot be realized without planning. The optimal physiological adaptation proceedings can only be reached through systematic and exactly controlled repetitions and loads, according to plan. Everything else is fraudulent to the athlete.

Fig. 38: Tommy Haas has also developed his own individual personality.

5 REALITY AND IDEAL PATHS IN TENNIS – A SUMMARY

5.1 SOME EXAMPLES OF FAULTY TALENT DEVELOPMENT

From the outset examples of the "burn-out" and "drop-out" effects have their foundation in faulty, non-systematic development. Long-term studies and analysis of hundreds of young players throughout Europe (SCHÖNBORN 1992) have pointed to this fact. There are principally two paths that may be followed, beginning with the very young players. On the one hand, even today it is found that the majority of young players followed the path of rapid and early tournament success. The other, better way, is the path of a patient, long-term, expert and systematic talent development. See Fig. 39 that illustrates both paths.

The path of a fast and early tournament success is shown in Fig. 39 through a black curve. Children who go along this path may be incorrectly led toward performance tennis through match playing success. Successful children will then automatically be referred to as potentially great or as future stars. Because these children (starting from 6/7 years of age) play predominantly or even solely tennis, they learn certain basic techniques very fast, with which they are soon able to operate, making relatively few mistakes.

Also, because children before puberty are relatively equal in size, speed, endurance and strength and because of their slow strokes and relatively small stroke repertory, by only allowing them to play simple tactics, where they will make the least number of mistakes, they should win regularly in tournaments which will help to boost their confidence and hence build for future success. And those are the children who already, at this age, play tennis over many years and many hours a week, have taken many training hours and have played in many tournaments per year. Our analysis has shown that a small number of ranked 10-11-year-olds play in 80-90 tournament matches per year! This is crazy, as not even the worlds no. 1 ranked adult player reaches a number near that, although through his timing, schedule and other obligations, both he and we think he has too large, unnatural and harmful tournament commitments in a year.

These children already miss, purely through time reasons (but not only), all basic training and basic fundamentals. They are the "famous" winners in the age categories 3 (under 14 years), 4 (under 12 years) and 5 (under 10 years). In the beginning their performance curve rises rapidly. Unfortunately, this wrong way is supported through the tournament system, the ranking list system and the resulting "promotional measures" as well as through over-ambitious parents and success hungry coaches and officials.

Around the age of 14 as a rule the first stagnation effects appear in these children. Because they are missing the actual and necessary coordination, conditioning and diverse technique training (they have no time for overall development due to the fact that all their time has been given over to playing tournaments and winning) soon after this they may start to lose against young players who have started tournament tennis much later and more discreetly but who are physically and technically better prepared and trained.

This period of stagnation lasts, as a rule, approx. two years. Thereafter, the second rise in performance begins (if they haven't lost interest because of failure or injury and have dropped out) and they reach their individual capacity limit around the age of 20 (see. Fig. 39).

And because they are not prepared for the high performance demand, they remain under their potential possibilities and sometimes can't even sustain their individual capacity limit very long. They normally break down rather rapidly and soon disappear within the multitude of nameless, average players.

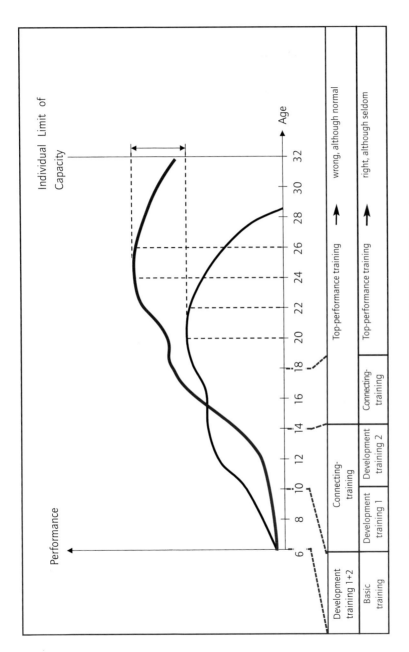

Fig. 39: Different performance developments (for more compare text; SCHÖNBORN 1989)

5.2 SOME ASPECTS OF CORRECT DEVELOPMENT

The patient and long-term path of a systematic talent development (See Fig. 39, coloured curve) runs differently. By the time children are about 12 years of age, their coordination development, the development of speed and tennis technique are of major importance. Thereby, neither tournament playing nor safe technique development can be pushed. For this reason, these children are among the losers. Their performance development up to approx. 13/14 years of age runs relatively slowly. Around the age of 14 to 15, however, the picture begins to change dramatically. Because these children have experienced an in depth basic training they are strong, fast and technically tennis-experienced.

On this basis, they begin to beat the former winners of the younger age groups. In addition, their performance curve develops steeply over a period of approx. two to three years and this performance growth stabilizes relatively fast.

After this phase, given the fact that training contents are correct, their performance curve continues developing and reaches its individual potential performance optimum, which lies much higher than that of the first group, around the ideal age for a tennis-player of approx. 23/26 years. Because of the excellent physical and technical basis, they can hold this performance level for a number of years and can even improve it. Above this, they are seldom prone to injuries, regenerate fast and are mentally strong.

One must emphasize the following, even though it may sound confusing; the influence of the general and specific motor and mental factors increases with increasing performance strength and the influence of the basic technique decreases.

In world top-class tennis and the broad world-class tennis, no essential differences in basic techniques exists among the individual players, with few exceptions. Countless players can serve at speeds of 190-200 km/h, have fast returns, or can hit perfect passing shots and volleys. The absolute top-class players in world tennis can use this stroke potential much more successfully and with greater variety. Their ability to act and react in difficult situations is much more pronounced. This is dependent upon two major factors:

1. They systematically train especially complicated situations, not only simple strokes and basic technique, but also conventional match play situations.
2. They are much better equipped in the coordination and conditioning areas and therefore able to master even the most difficult motoric situations.

For these reasons they are more self-confident and mentally stronger, which means that they owe their playing ability to perfect physical skill and mental strength and not so much for having better technical "super weapons". If they do have them, then for the reason that they were able to develop and perfect coordination and physical conditioning, whereby the importance of the complexity in training is substantiated.

CLOSING WORDS

5.3

Both authors realize that the path toward becoming a champion in tennis, as written in this book, is more a characterization of a few really top-class stars than of the majority of the tennis talents world-wide who are doomed to fail because of incompetent coaching and on the basis of lacking professional knowledge. This was the reason we have decided to show future talents, their coaches, parents and officials a logically based description for an optimal path toward becoming a top-notch player. The path described in this book is not only based upon the latest knowledge of sport science but also upon more than forty years of national and international practical tennis experience of coaching and working with youth and top-class sports.

We hope and wish that this book finds wide consent in professional circles, even if the contents, for some, may demand a radical change in thinking. A child is not a "small adult" and he is no guinea pig on which it is possible to practice the art of improvising, widely spread in the game of tennis. Children and adolescents trust adults and place themselves confidently under their guardianship. It is therefore our responsibility to give the next generation the best quality of work and to offer them a path of development that leads to success. What each person makes out of this possibility is dependent upon very many factors, which, for the greatest part have to be sought in the personality of the young players.

A possible failure or not reaching the desired goals should never lie with the professionals training the child! And it certainly doesn't speak for the quality of the professionals if for example parents think they understand more about the matter than the professionals involved. Raising children and adolescents is a very difficult and responsible task. Adults are responsible for the coming generation and that is why we have to set our relationship with this generation to a high level of quality. That also pertains to sport, in this case, tennis. We hope, with this book, we have made a small contribution and wish all readers much success through it and above all, lots of fun and success in daily training.

LITERATURE

ASMUS, A.S.: Physische und motorische Entwicklung im Kindes- und Jugend-alter. Kassel 1991.

BUSCHMANN, J.: Ausdauertraining für Kinder. Aachen 1986.

DEUTSCHER TENNIS-BUND (Hrsg.): Tennis-Lehrplan. Bd. 1. München 1995, 7. Aufl.; Bd. 2. München 1996, 7. Aufl.

EHLENZ, H./GROSSER, M./ZIMMERMANN, E.: Krafttraining. München 1998, 6. Aufl.

FERRAUTI, A./MAIER, P./WEBER, K.: Tennis-Training mit System. Niedernhausen 1996.

FRÖHNER, G.: Die Belastbarkeit als zentrale Größe im Nachwuchstraining. Münster 1993.

FRÖHNER, G.: Physiologische Grundlagen der Belastbarkeitssicherung. In: HELD, C. et al. (Red.): Sport ist Spitze. (11. Intern. Workshop, Dortmund 1996) Krefeld 1997, 53-76.

GROSSER, M.: Schnelligkeitstraining. München 1991.

GROSSER, M./KRAFT, H./SCHÖNBORN, R.: Speed Training in Tennis. Aachen 2000.

GROSSER, M./STARISCHKA, S.: Das neue Konditionstraining. München 1998, 7. Aufl.

HEINZEL/KOCH/STARKER JAHN: Koordinationstraining im Tennis. DTB-Trainerbibliothek. Sindelfingen 1997.

HIRTZ, P. et al.: Koordinative Fähigkeiten im Schulsport. Berlin 1985.

HOLLMANN, W. et al.: Prävention und Rehabilitation von Herzkreislauf-krankheiten durch körperliches Training. Stuttgart 1983.

HOLLMANN, W./HETTINGER, TH.: Sportmedizin. Stuttgart 2000, 4. Aufl.

HOSSNER, E.-J.: Prinzipien des Techniktrainings im Spitzensport. In: ROTH, K. (Hrsg.): Techniktraining im Spitzensport. Köln 1996, 84-99.

KOINZER, K.: Energetischer Metabolismus und dessen hormonelle Steuerung bei Kindern und Jugendlichen. In: Medizin und Sport 27 (1987) 7, 208-210.

MARTIN, D. et al.: Handbuch Kinder- und Jugendtraining. Schorndorf 1999.

NEUMAIER, A.: Koordinatives Anforderungsprofil und Koordinationstraining. Köln 1999.

PIAGET J.: Genetische Erkenntnistheorie. Frankfurt/M. 1972.

ROWLAND, T.W.: Development Aspects of Physiological Function Relating to Aerobic Exercise in Children. In: Sports Medicine 10 (1990), 255-266.

SCHÖNBORN, R.: Positive und negative Leistungsentwicklung im Tennis. Vortrag bei ITF World Wide Workshop 1989.

SCHÖNBORN, R.: Advanced Techniques for Competitive Tennis. Aachen 1999.

SCHÖNBORN, R.: Vortrag A-Trainerausbildung Tennis. Halle 1999.

SCHÖNBORN/KRAFT: Handbuch für Tennistrainer. Grasleben 1998.

SCHNEIDER, H./SCHÖNBORN, R.: Koordinationstraining im Tennis. Video. DTB 1995.

WUTSCHERK, H./SCHMIDT, H./KÖTHE, R.: Körperbautypologisch- und altersbedingte Differenzierungen von Körperbaumerkmalen. In: Medizin und Sport 25 (1985), 143-148.Sachwortverzeichnis

PHOTO AND ILLUSTRATION CREDITS

Cover Photo: Bongarts Sportfotografie, Hamburg
Photos: Jochen Körner, Hamburg
Drawings: Ernst-Peter Zeuch, Seesen
Cover Design: Birgit Engelen, Stolberg

INDEX

INDEX

INDEX

Meyer & Meyer:

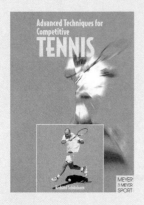

Alistair Higham

Momentum: The Hidden Force in Tennis

Momentum – the Hidden Force in Tennis is about the battle of competitive tennis matches – the ebbs and flows, the turning points, why momentum switches and how and when to use your skills to gain control. It is also an enjoyable read, both thought provoking and original.

86 pages
Two-colour print
Various photos
Paperback, 14.8 x 21 cm
ISBN 1-84126-040-1
£ 9.95 UK/$ 14.95 US/
$ 20.95 CDN/€ 14.90

Richard Schönborn

Advanced Techniques for Competitive Tennis

Former Davis Cup player and highly experienced coach Richard Schönborn thinks the methods used for decades to train technique in tennis are lagging behind other sports. In this book Schönborn sets out to change the way tennis is taught and coached by making technique training more relevant to what happens in a match. The book provides a detailed analysis of technique and how it is learned, then places technique training into the context of an overall tennis training programme.

2nd edition
280 pages, Full colour,
170 figures
Paperback, 14.8 x 21 cm
ISBN 1-84126-046-0
£ 17.95 UK/$ 29.00 US/
$ 39.95 CDN/€ 22.90

MEYER & MEYER Verlag | Von-Coels-Straße 390 | D-52080 Aachen, Germany | Fax + +49 (0)2 41/9 58 10-10

the Expert in Tennis

Manfred Grosser/Heinz Kraft
Richard Schönborn
**Speed Training for
Tennis**

Although speed is, along with technique and coordination, one of the most important performance-limiting factors in tennis, apart from a few exceptions it is mentioned only sporadically if at all in the specialist tennis literature. The authors of this book have been very active in this and other areas for decades, and set out the whole problem of speed in a systematic and tennis-specific way.

136 pages
Two-colour print
Many photos and illustrations
Paperback, 14.8 x 21 cm
ISBN 1-84126-030-4
£ 9.95 UK/$ 14.95 US/
$ 20.95 CDN/€ 14.90

Lutz Steinhöfel
**Training Exercises
for Competitive Tennis**

„Training Exercises for Competitive Tennis" provides the tennis coach with a detailed overview of up-to-date training exercises for competitive tennis. A broad spectrum of over 150 exercise lessons with numerous variations are displayed in more than 70 diagrams, together with notes and commentary. All the exercises are suited for any player as an individual training programme for any of these combinations.

176 pages
85 photos, many figures
Paperback, 14.8 x 2 cm
ISBN 3-89124-464-9
£ 12.95 UK/$ 17.95 US/
$ 25.95 CDN/€ 16.90

MEYER & MEYER Verlag ¦ Von-Coels-Straße 390 ¦ D-52080 Aachen, Germany ¦ Fax + +49 (0)2 41/9 58 10-10

X02G Anz2 02/02

Health

Georg Neumann
Nutrition in Sport

The book makes recommendations for physiologically useful dietary planning before, during and after training in various sports. It also examines risk-prone groups in sports nutrition. The emphasis is on presenting the latest research on the effects of carbohydrates and proteins and other active substances, such as vitamins and minerals, on performance training. Particular attention is paid to the intake of food and fluids under special conditions such as training in heat, in the cold and at high altitudes.

208 pages, Two-colour print
Some full-colour photos
Paperback, 14.8 x 21 cm
ISBN 1-84126-003-7
£ 12.95 UK/$ 17.95 US/
$ 25.95 CDN/€ 18.90

MEYER & MEYER SPORT

MEYER & MEYER Verlag | Von-Coels-Straße 390 | D-52080 Aachen, Germany | Fax +49 (0)2 41 / 9 58 10-10

X02G An3 02/02